Stonewall Jackson
Loved in the South; Admired in the North

"Look!" cried General Bee. "There are Jackson and his men standing like a stone wall. Rally behind them!"

In the battle that followed, Jackson lifted his left hand high and moved back and forth shouting encouragement to his men. At a critical moment, he spurred his horse, Little Sorrel, into the center of his regiment and shouted, "Reserve your fire until they come within fifty yards. Then fire and give them the bayonet. And when you charge, yell like the furies."

Weeks before, the men had practiced the blood-curdling yell of *woh-who-ey*. This combination of Apache war whoop, wolf howl and panther scream had a terrifying effect. The Federals broke rank, threw down their weapons and fled.

Stonewall's fearlessness had begun years earlier when he climbed the highest tree in pursuit of a coon, and when he determined to learn in spite of being called the school dummy and school charity case.

Even at West Point his grades nearly scraped the bottom in his first year. But he worked hard and raised his level each year until he graduated in the upper third of his class. An official later remarked, "If the course at West Point had been a year longer, Jackson would have graduated at the head of his class."

A Northern newspaper mourned his death: "Stonewall Jackson was a great general, a noble Christian and a pure man."

ABOUT THE AUTHOR

Charles Ludwig, son of missionaries, grew up in Kenya. He has traveled in scores of countries and preached in many of them. His writings include one thousand articles, stories and serials, and over forty books. In 1979 he received a National Religious Book Award for his book on Michael Faraday.

Author Ludwig especially enjoyed writing this biography of Stonewall Jackson. He says his interest in the War Between the States began in childhood with his grandfather telling about hearing the guns of Gettysburg. As a grown man he visited Gettysburg and many other battle sites, and he stands in awe of strong and godly men like Robert E. Lee and Stonewall Jackson. They were winning losers, he says, and he wants to transmit that feeling to readers of this book.

ABOUT THE ARTIST

Michael L. Denman says he has always liked to draw. He remembers that in his poor family paper was scarce. So his grandmother gave him her Christmas cards, which in those days were folded into fourths. Michael unfolded them and was delighted to have full sheets of paper, blank on one side, ready for his drawings. His favorite books as a child were those on history, so he especially likes to illustrate history books for today's children. He reads each book before illustrating it and his children read it too. They enjoy talking together about the history books.

Mr. Denman at first learned most of his art skills by himself, but later he studied art at Cooper Institute. For more than ten years he has illustrated children's storybooks, workbooks and readers, as well as visual aids that teachers use. He is an Art Director at McCallum Design Company and lives with his wife and family in North Ridgeville, Ohio.

Stonewall Jackson

Loved in the South; Admired in the North

by

Charles Ludwig

illustrated by

Michael Denman

For Pastor E. B. and Marian Jones who have extended a perpetual West Virginia welcome to us during the last half century.

COPYRIGHT © 1989 by Mott Media, Inc.

Kurt Dietsch, Cover Artist

LIBRARY OF CONGRESS CATALOGING IN PUBLICATION DATA

Ludwig, Charles, 1918-
  Stonewall Jackson; Loved in the South; admired in the North / by Charles Ludwig.

    p.   cm.—(Sowers Series)
    Bibliography: p. 181
    Includes index.

    SUMMARY: A biography of the Confederate general who gained the nickname Stonewall for his stand at the first batle of Bull Run during the Civil War.
    ISBN 0-88062-157-5
    1. Jackson, Stonewall, 1824-1863—Juvenile literature.
2. Generals—United States—Biography—Juvenile literature.
3. Confederate States of America. Army—Biography—Juvenile literature. 4. United State. Army—Biography—Juvenile literature. 5. United States—History—Civil War, 1861-1865-Campaigns—Juvenile literature. [1. Jackson, Stonewall, 1824-1863. 2. Generals. 3. United States—History—Civil War, 1861-1865.]   I. Title. II. Series: Sowers.
E467.1.J15L83   1989   973.7'3'0924—dc 19 [B] [92]   89-3097
                                                        CIP AC

ISBN 0-88062-157-5   Paperbound

CONTENTS

1

A Boy, A Fishing Pole And Memories

Perched on a stump facing the creek with his fishing pole by his side, nine-year-old Tom was certain that he was the most miserable boy who had ever lived. Others could return home to their parents. Not he! Both were dead. His father, Jonathan Jackson, had died when Tom was not quite three.

The *real* memory of that occasion was dim; but having heard it repeated many times, it had seared into his brain with the clarity of the C-brand on one of Uncle Cummin's steers.

Now as he glanced at his fishing line and bobber, those grim days shuddered back into dreadful reality. His sister Elizabeth had been stricken by typhoid. Day after day his parents lingered at her side. They gave her the prescribed medicines, and kept a cool cloth on her forehead. Even so, she continued to sink. Finally, she closed her eyes for the last time. Tears streaked his cheeks as they lowered the homemade coffin into the oblong cavity dug into the earth.

Liz had been a wonderful sister. Sobbing out loud, he knew he would never forget her.

Then two weeks after her death, his father succumbed to typhoid. After twenty days of intense struggle, he uttered a sigh and was gone.

"Father's now with Elizabeth in Heaven," comforted his mother, as they slowly made their way from the cemetery to their Clarksburg home. Tom never forgot the emptiness of that house when he first stepped inside.

The day after Tom's father died, Dr. James McCally pounded the snow from his boots at the door.

Tom was curious as this man who had eased him into the world removed his tall hat and lifted out the stethoscope. "Maybe you'd better go and play," he suggested. "Your ma isn't feeling well."

Reluctantly, Tom slipped on his oversized boots and meandered down the muddy street. Inspired, he rolled a huge ball of snow and made a snowman on an empty lot. After it was completed, he returned home. "Go and play some more," ordered McCally, pounding his fist into his hand. "Your older brother, Warren, was here just a few minutes ago, and I told him to go and look for you. He went that way." The doctor pointed in the direction where Tom had built the snowman.

Minutes later Tom found Warren lingering by a vacant lot. "Doc McCally was sure anxious to get rid of us," greeted Warren.

"I didn't know that Ma was sick."

Warren started to say something, and then changed his mind.

"I hope Ma isn't going to die," said Tom, shaking his head.

"She's not going to die!" assured Warren with a

knowing look. "Ma's going to have a baby."

"How do you know?" Tom's jaw sagged.

"Because I remember how McCally came when you were born. He was wearing that same stovepipe hat."

"Did he have that forked thing he puts around his neck?"

"He sure did. And I saw him take it out of his hat and attach it to his ears. You were born real close to midnight on the 20th or 21st of January, 1824. But since Pa forgot to wind the clock, we never knew whether you were born on the 20th or 21st."

Tom laughed. "Maybe I should celebrate two birthdays every year."

Later, McCally met them at the door. He was smiling. "The Lord has sent you a new sister," he announced.

"What's her name?" asked Tom anxiously.

"Better ask your ma."

"Her name is Laura Ann," replied their mother. "Come close and have a look."

Tom scowled at the little pink face. "Ugh!" he exclaimed. "She's as red as a red cherry."

"And so were you when you were born," replied his mother.

"Give her time. She'll soon be as white as either of you."

Tom laughed. "She's all right," he agreed with reluctance, "But she's not like Liz".

His mother smiled.

Tom remembered how Laura Ann had both whitened and gained weight, and how he was finally allowed to hold her for the first time. Life was again running smoothly. Then while picking up a ball from behind the door, he accidentally overheard his mother confiding to a neighbor.

"Jonathan was a fine man," she said. Her voice was broken and he could tell she was crying. "But he was too generous. He was always signing notes for others. When they skipped the country, he had to make good for them. He lost his entire inheritance. Every cent! Even this nice brick home belongs to the bank. It only has three rooms because Jonthan had hoped that when his business prospered he could use it for offices and build a larger home nearby. I've been stripped of everything. . . . We'll soon be out on the street. It's terrible to be penniless."

As Tom sat thinking of these events, his bobber suddenly went straight down and he was shaken back into the present. Scrambling to his feet, he grabbed the pole and started winding in the string. The catch

was so heavy the pole bent. Slowly, slowly he pulled in more of the string. By the weight, he was almost certain that he had a pike. His eyes on the water, he became even more careful. Once before he had been in too big a hurry, and just as the glistening pike emerged from the water, the string broke and the pike, a huge one, went off with his hook. Now, extremely cautious, he kept pulling in the line inch by inch. Then his heart sank. His catch was nothing but a turtle! He detached the hook and tossed the oval thing back into the water. A glance at the sun indicated that it was time to return home. As he trudged along without a single fish to show for an afternoon's work his mind again returned to the past.

After his mother had lost their snug little house, some friends provided her with a one-room cottage. This meant that all four of them were confined to a single room. But they got used to it; and a few weeks later his mother was hired to teach in a private school. This work, plus what she earned with a needle, enabled her to pay all the bills.

One day after two years of this type of living, Tom's mother made a sudden announcement at the table. It was an announcement that he never forgot.

"I have news for you," she said.

"Is it *good* news?" asked Warren.

"I think so," She smiled broadly.

"Then what is it?" demanded Tom.

"I'm going to get married."

"Married!" exclaimed Tom and Warren almost together.

"Yes, we're going to be married. Captain Blake Woodson will be your step-father. Like your pa, he's a lawyer."

"But he's much older than you," objected Warren as he put a dab of applesauce on his toast. "Where will we live?"

"We've thought about that. Some of *his* children are already grown and have families of their own. His smaller children will move in with relatives."

"And what will happen to us?" asked Tom, his blue eyes alight with wonder.

"The Lord will direct."

"Are you sure?" Warren was a little abrupt.

"It seems that your new father will have a job in Fayette County, and if he does we'll be moving down there. Since you are already ten, Warren, we've decided to let you live with your Uncle Neale in Wood County, Ohio. Tom and Laura Ann will stay with us."

Brokenhearted, for he and Warren were very close, Tom burst into tears and fled outside. "It isn't fair," he wailed.

Julia and Captain Blake settled in a little house near Ansted in Fayette County.

Tom continued to relive the past while he walked along the creek. He remembered that neither he nor Laura liked the little house in which they were crammed. Also, it was sort of scary living in the mountains, and there was no adequate school for him to attend. Then one evening his mother said to him, "The Lord is sending you a little half-brother or half-sister. That means we'll be rather crowded."

"And so?" Tom held his breath.

"And so we've decided that you and Laura will move up north and live with Aunt Brake."

"And who's she?" demanded Tom a little angrily.

"She's your father's sister."

"But, Ma, Laura and I don't want to leave you, even though we hate it down here. I could sleep on the floor."

"And neither do I want you to leave me." She wiped her eyes. "But there is absolutely no other way."

Tom remembered he was wedged in the crook of an apple tree when the man he suspected of being Uncle Brake galloped up on a white horse. Carefully, Tom eased himself out of the tree and slipped up behind the stranger to make certain who he was.

The moment his mother faced the heavy-set man and asked, "So you've come for the children?" Tom fled. While hiding in the woods, he heard both his mother and the stranger calling, "Tom! Tom! Where are you?"

As the voices kept getting closer, Tom crept deeper and deeper into the little clump of forest. Then he heard a third voice, "Tom, supper's ready. There ain't no use for you to be scared. Nobody's gonna hurt you nohow." This new voice sounded like that of a slave. *What was he to do?* He didn't want to frighten his mother by hiding out. Moreover, he had heard that there were mean wolves in this neighborhood. Also, it was getting cold, and he was hungry.

Creeping back to the house, he slipped inside.

"This is your Uncle Brake," announced his mother.

Tom glanced at the man out of the corners of his eyes. Then, burying his head in his mother's lap, he sobbed, "But Ma I don't want to leave you."

Brake forced a smile. "You'll like it up our way. We have a big mill, and we're just a few miles from Clarksburg."

"I still don't want to leave." He dug his fists into his eyes.

"You can have a lot of fun at our place. You'll be able to go coon huntin', and there are lots of buffalo around."

Eventually after Uncle Brake had given him a jack-knife and a pocketbook, he agreed to leave his mother and go north. Early the next morning after a heavy breakfast of bacon and eggs and pancakes, Tom and Laura kissed their mother goodbye. Then Tom swung onto Uncle Robinson's horse. (He was the slave who'd called for Tom in the woods). Next, Laura mounted Uncle Brake's horse. Tom waved until his mother was out of sight, then his eyes overflowed with a fresh burst of tears.

"There's no use for you to cry," comforted Uncle Robinson. "Your ma's gonna have a baby. You'll be a helpin' her by livin' wid de Brakes."

Jackson's Mill has been properly named. A dozen miles southwest of Clarksburg, it was thick with Jacksons. The first mill was built as far back as 1799. It was a place of activity and Tom enjoyed watching people coming in to get their grain turned into flour. But he kept thinking about his mother; and each evening as he said his prayer at the side of his bed, he visualized her standing at the door. Her dark gray eyes, brown hair, and slim body were as real as life. He was confident that she was the best mother in the whole world.

Tom realized that his Aunt and Uncle Brake were doing all they could for him. But sometimes he and his Uncle disagreed. Eventually, he decided to run away. A long time before, he had heard about his Uncle Cummins, and he made up his mind that he would move in with him.

After knocking at the door of his father's cousin, Judge Jackson, in Clarksburg, he said to the Judge's wife, "Auntie, I'm starved. May I have something to eat?"

While attempting to hide her astonishment, his aunt warmed leftovers and placed them before him. As he gobbled them up, he confesssed, "Uncle Brake and I don't agree. I've left him."

"Oh, but the Brakes really love you."

"Maybe they do. But Uncle Brake and I can't get along."

"Mmmm, maybe after a night's sleep and a good breakfast you'll change your mind."

"Never! I've quit him and I shall not return."

"All right. All right. I know a lot of Jacksons, and they're all as stubborn as mules." She laughed.

The next morning after breakfast, Tom left Clarksburg. He continued on in the general direction of his grandfather's home in Lewis County, a solid eighteen miles west of his birthplace. As he made his way over the frozen roads, he became so weary he was tempted to give up. But thoughts of living with Uncle Cummins, his father's colorful half brother now living on his grandfather's farm, spurred him on. It was late in the afternoon when he finally stumbled up to his uncle's door.

"And where have you come from?" demanded his uncle after he had pulled him into the house. Before Tom could reply, he added, "Before you answer, you'd better have something to eat. All Jacksons are tough. Even so, they have to eat!"

"Uncle Brake and I couldn't get along, and so I decided to move in with you."

"Wise boy! Wise boy! But did you know that your ma is very sick. Heard from Captain Blake yesterday. He said if we want to see her alive we'd better hurry down to Fayette County at once. We're leaving tomorrow."

2

The Struggles Of An Orphan

Tom felt his heart thumping as he dismounted near the front door of his mother's house. After tying his horse to the fence, he knocked at the door.

"How's ma?" he demanded the moment Blake opened the door.

"She's not doing very well. The doctor is in with her now."

Their conversation was interrupted by the cry of a baby.

"What's that?" asked Tom.

"Have you forgotten that you have a new half brother?" asked Blake as he cradled the baby in his arms.

"What's his name?" Tom was apprehensive.

"Don't you know?"

Tom shook his head.

"His name is William Wirt Woodson."

Suddenly the door to Julia's bedroom opened and the doctor emerged.

"How's she doing?" asked the captain.

"Not so well. If God doesn't step in, I'm afraid that we've lost her."

Dabbing at his eyes, Tom rushed to his mother's side. "I'm afraid my time has come," wheezed his mother. "You'd better call Warren and Laura so that I can have a last word with them."

As the children gathered around her bed, she took Tom by the hand, and then with great emphasis she said, "I'm expecting each of you to amount to something. Someday you will also be called Home. When that time comes, may it be said that the world is better because you lived." She shifted her head on the pillow. "The secret of living right is to stay close to the Lord. You must learn to pray. Pray when you go to bed. Pray when you get up. Pray during the day. And have faith! You must believe in the One who made you." Exhausted, she closed her eyes. Several minutes later she opened them and slowly looked around the room.

"I have a feeling that my time on earth is short. Pray for me and promise that you'll be good to one another."

A few minutes later she made a sigh and was gone.

Tom's step-father remembered those last moments well. He remarked, "She had a clear mind until she died. She met her fate without a murmur or struggle. No Christian on earth, no matter what evidence he might have had of a happy hereafter, could have died with more fortitude."

Following the funeral, Tom, along with Laura and Warren, mounted their horses and started north to Cummins' place. It was a long lonesome ride, especially for Tom. Never in his seven years did he feel as forsaken as he did right then. *Was life worth living?* His mother had said it was, and he believed

her. He just knew that she was right, for she always
had been.

Tom had barely emerged from these ever-so-vivid
memories when he reached his Uncle Cummins'
place.

As he was putting his fishing pole away, Cummins
appeared in the doorway with a barrel of flour under
each arm. "Did you bring us some fish?" he asked
with a doubtful grin.

"Naw. All I caught was a miserable turtle, and I
threw him back into the creek."

"Too bad," laughed his broad-shouldered uncle.
"My taster was hungry for fish. Never mind. I shot
a deer. We'll have venison for supper." He parked
both barrels of flour by the fireplace, hoisted a barrel
of cider to his lips and took a long drink out of the
bunghole.

Tom shook his head. "How do you do that?"

"I can do *that* because I'm six feet tall. That means
that I'm half a foot taller than your pa. Also, I can
manage because I was raised on buffalo. Buffalo meat
makes a man strong—especially if he has Jackson
blood!" He put the barrel in a safe place and slapped
his thighs. "Jackson blood is mighty good blood."

Tom enjoyed living with Cummins. His Uncle
taught him how to oversee the slaves when they
worked in the fields and cleared new land. He also
taught him to milk, shoot rabbits, and go coon
hunting. The baying of the dogs as they chased and
treed the coons became the finest music he'd ever
heard. During one famous hunt, several of the hunters
felt assured that the dogs had treed a bear rather than
a coon.

"I wouldn't climb that tree," warned one of the
older men.

"Why not?" asked Tom.

"Because that ain't no coon up thar."

"Then, what is it?"

"It's a ba'r!"

Tom laughed. "I'm not afraid," he said as he boldly hoisted himself onto the lowest limb. Up, up he climbed.

The crowd below kept shouting, "Be keerful, Tom."

Ignoring his advisors, Tom kept working himself higher and higher. As he moved from one branch to another, Cummins shouted, "Tom, you're takin' your life in your own hands. Be mighty keerful."

Ignoring the warnings, Tom pulled himself into an even higher branch. Then he got hold of the base of the narrow limb on which the coon was clinging. "Well, Mr. Coon, I think you've had it," he said, as he gave the limb a mighty shake. Seconds later, the coon went tumbling down.

The dogs were ready.

After Tom had descended, his uncle wrapped his arms around him. "Weren't you skeered?" he demanded.

"Skeered! What's that?"

By the time he was ten, Tom was an expert fisherman. Indeed, he became such an expert the neighbors depended on him to supply fish for their tables. The nearby West Fork became his favorite place. One evening as he was returning home, Colonel Talbott stopped him.

You have some mighty fine fish," observed the distinguished veteran of the War of 1812.

"Yes, Sir. The Lord was mighty good to me."

"How 'bout sellin' me that pike?"

"Sorry. I've already promised it to Mr. Kester."

"How much will he pay for it?"

"Fifty cents."

"That's a mighty big pike for only fifty cents. Tell you what—" He eyed the nearly three-foot fish greedily. "Tell you what. I'll give you seventy-five cents for it."

"Sorry." Tom started to walk away.

"Don't be in a hurry, boy. We're havin' company and the missus could use that fish. Since I knew your pa, I'll go the limit. I'll give you a dollar."

"A whole dollar?" Tom licked his lips. A dollar was a small fortune. It would more than pay for a good pair of pants. While he hesitated, Talbott began to count out the money.

Tom was on the verge of yielding when he remembered his last moments with his mother. She had told him to make his life count, and he knew that he could not make his life count if he didn't keep his word. "Sorry," he replied, "that fish is already sold." He adjusted his load of fish and started to walk away.

"Just a minute, youngun' " cried the Colonel, "I'll do a little better. How about a dollar and a quarter?"

Tom studied the man's face and then glanced at the fish. A dollar and a quarter was more money that he had ever seen at one time. It was better than a week's wages. He was about to say yes, when his mind returned again to his mother's deathbed.

"Sorry," he replied. "I just can't do it. You see Colonel Talbott, my ma taught me that people should be able to count on my word. Maybe I'll get another fish tomorrow, and if I do I'll sell you that one."

As Tom returned to his uncle's place, he felt a surge of happiness he had never before experienced. Suddenly he found himself singing a hymn the Methodists had been using in their camp meetings. Stepping in rhythm to the words, he made the woods echo with:

> *Amazing Grace! how sweet the sound,*
> *That saved a wretch like me,*
> *I once was lost, but now am found,*
> *Was blind, but now I see.*

That evening as Tom squeezed lemon juice onto his helping of fish, he was so happy it seemed that he had acquired wings and could fly. That night he found it hard to sleep. Memories of his mother kept coming before him. It seemed that he could almost see her smiling at him from heaven. He remembered the advice she had given him as she struggled with death. "Pray when you go to bed and pray when you get up and pray during the day," she had said. This he had done. But he also remembered that whenever they ate, she always asked the Lord to bless the food. Uncle Cummins never did any of these things. Thinking about this, he resolved that he would silently ask the Lord to bless his food at each meal even though the others did not.

The next morning after he had mentally asked the Lord to bless his food at breakfast, he said, "Uncle Cummins, I've been worried because I'm not going to school." He poured some of the maple syrup he had tapped on his pancakes. "I've heard that Phillip Cox, Jr. is going to open a place of learning next month. W-would it be all right with you if I attended?"

"Of course it will be all right. I didn't git any eddication 'cause I had to work. But I'm all for eddication. My uncle, George Jackson, was a member of Congress. He was elected because he had an eddication."

"Am I related to him?" Tom's eyes widened.

"Of course. And let me tell you somethin' interestin' 'bout him. While he was in Congress, he

got to know Andy Jackson. At that time Andy was
a representative from Tennessee.''

"Do you mean the one who is now president of the
United States?'' gasped Tom, his eyes even wider.

"I do. And let me tell you somethin' even better.
Uncle George became a good friend of his. One day
as they were talkin' 'bout their distant relatives, they
discovered that some of their ancestors on both sides
had been neighbors in Ireland!''

"Could it be then that I—Tom Jackson—am
related to our president?''

"You may be.''

Suddenly Tom's throat was dry. Overwhelmed, he
tried to say something, but all he could squeeze out
was a loud "Wow!''

Cummins laughed. "Uncle George isn't the only
important relative we have. There are a lot of others.
I'll tell you about some of 'em at another time. But
now I have to go and look at a farm I'm thinkin' of
buyin'.''

As a result of Cummins' recommendation, Tom
enrolled in Phillip Cox's school. Entering the shack
where the children were gathering, he had a curious
feeling that an important new door was opening for
him. Tom was only six when Andrew Jackson ran for
his second term in 1832, but he remembered hearing
the grown-ups talking about it. From what they said,
Andy must have had a colorful childhood.

Like himself, Andy had been born in poverty.
Indeed, his father died even *before* he was born, and
his mother died of "prison fever" which she acquired
by tending American soldiers who were captured by
the British during the Revolution. Next, an older
brother was killed in the war, and another died of
smallpox while he was being held by the British. Andy,
himself, at the age of fourteen, was captured by the

Redcoats. When a British officer asked him to shine his shoes, Andy refused. This so angered the officer, he struck him with his sword and cut his arm to the bone.

When Tom thought about these things, he felt goose bumps scoot down his spine.

But, although he tingled in knowing that he had brave blood in his veins he knew he would have to go to school. On the day school opened, he took a seat on the first split-log in front.

Tom felt a little nervous because most of the students were younger than he; and also because many of them had better clothes than he had. His pants had a huge patch in the seat.

"This morning we're going to learn the letters of the alphabet," said Cox, smiling at everyone. "Our English alphabet has twenty-six letters. These letters are: a, b, c, d, and so on. Each letter has a different pronunciation than the others. This morning, we're going to learn the first five letters."

Holding up her hand, Sally, the daughter of a rich farmer, said, "I already know all of that!"

"And so do I," cried several others.

Tom inwardly groaned.

"Very well," said Cox, rubbing the top of his shiny bald head. "But there are others who don't know their letters and so you'll have to be patient with them." Pointing to Tom, he asked, "Do you know them?"

"I'm afraid, Sir, I do not." As he spoke, Tom felt a hollow place forming in his stomach.

"Very well. Then for Tom's sake as well as for the others like him, we will start with the letter: *a*."

"Ohhhhh," groaned several.

Cox held up his hand. "Those who already know the alphabet, raise your hands."

Everyone raised a hand except Tom and two other boys.

Cox paced back and forth two or three times in deep thought, then he said, "I'm glad for all of you who are ahead. Nonetheless, you'll have to be patient with the others. I want us all to work together. In a short time, those who are behind will catch up."

Ignoring another chorus of groans, Cox held up a card with the letter *a* on it. "This is the first letter of the alphabet," he said. "Sometimes it is pronounced *ah* as in ma. At other times it is pronounced *aye* as in day or pay or say.'' Holding the card up in front of Tom, he asked, ''How would you, Master Jackson, pronounce it?''

All at once Tom felt his ears reddening and sweat forming on his forehead. He stared at the card, and as he stared he felt that every eye in the room was boring a hole into the back of his head. ''It-it-is p-p-p-prounced. . . . Oh, Sir, I've forgotten.''

''Class, how is *a* pronounced?''

''It is pronounced *ah* as in *ma,* or *aye* as in *day* or *pay* or *say*,'' replied Sally.

''Now tell us, Master Tom, how is *a* pronounced.''

''Sir, it is pronounced *ah* as in *ma*, or *aye* as in, or *aye* as in—'' Tom felt his ears reddening again and a fresh dampness forming on his forehead and neck. ''I'm sorry, sir, I've plumb forgotten.''

''Dummy!'' exploded Sally in a loud whisper.

''None of that!'' cautioned the teacher. ''Tom Jackson is a fine boy, and I know he'll learn in time.''

''But while he's learnin' the rest of ussun's are wastin' our time and it's a-costin' us three cents a day to come here. My pa says three cents is a lot of money,'' replied Sally angrily.

''It shore is,'' agreed her older sister Barbara. ''Three cents will buy a dozen eggs.''

By the time school let out, Tom was so humiliated he felt like never going back again. But on his way home he remembered that there was a possibility, just a faint possibility that he might, just might, be related to President Andy Jackson himself.

That thought lifted his spirits.

3

'Readin', 'Ritin'
And 'Rithmetic

"How was school?" asked Cummins as he poured himself a large glass of buttermilk.

"Oh, it was all right," replied Tom. He stared at his plate which was filled with breaded trout.

"You're not very enthusiastic. Did you learn anything?"

"Uncle, tell me some more about President Jackson," evaded Tom, obviously changing the subject.

"What do you want to know about him?" Cummins frowned.

"You told me they called him Old Hickory. Why did he get such a name?"

His uncle laughed and helped himself to more fish. "He got the name in the War of 1812. In 1813 Jackson offered President Madison the services of 2500 men. His offer was accepted and he along with this men were sent to Natchez, Mississippi." Cummins wiped his mouth.

"Go on," urged Tom.

"While Jackson was organizin' his men," continued Cummins as he worked out a bone in the tail-part of his fish, "he got an order to dismiss his men and send 'em home." His uncle knelt on the floor to give the cat some milk.

"Go on, Uncle Cummins. And so what did he do?"

"Wal, Jackson weren't no man to be pushed around. And so—" Cummins refilled his glass with buttermilk.

"And so?" begged Tom.

"You'd better eat. Your food is gettin' cold."

Tom took a nibble of fish. "And so?"

"And so Jackson defied the order and marched his men back to Tennessee. He was especially angry because none of them had been paid. His soldiers were delighted. While one of 'em was a-talkin' about Jackson, he muttered, 'He's as tough as Old Hickory.' That, Tom, is how he got that colorful name."

Tom sighed. "And just think, Uncle, Old Hickory was once just an orphan like me," he said, shaking his head and attacking his fish. "But tell me, Uncle, how did Old Hickory get to be President Jackson?"

"He became President because he made himself a hero by winnin' the Battle of New Orleans. Yes, Tom, Jackson was a great man and we're related to him. But now I'll have to leave you. Have to get some papers ready so I can see my lawyer tomorrow. Some of the land titles in this county are quite unreliable."

Tom felt better when he left for his second day of school.

Although he was far behind, he was convinced that he would manage to at least learn the alphabet. That confidence put a spring in his step.

Tom took his seat on the front row and eagerly awaited the beginning of the lesson. Teacher Cox smiled at him from behind the vertical section of log that he used for a desk. "Now, Master Tom," he said. "What are the two ways in which the letter *a* is pronounced?"

Rising to his feet, Tom said, "*A* can be pronounced *ah* as in *pa* or it can be pronounced *a* as in *jay*, *ray*—or even *bay*. A is also the first . . ."

"That ain't right," broke in Sally. "You taught us that *a* rhymes with *aye* as in *day* or *pay* or *say*."

Humiliated, Tom stared at the floor.

While all the girls laughed, Cox said, "You are both right. But I think Tom's answer was far the best. For you see Tom had a *new* idea. Anyone can repeat what someone else says. That is easy. Tom Jackson, like President Jackson, has shown that he has *real* talent."

The teacher's comments ended the laughter, and Tom felt as confident as he had felt when he shook the coon out of the tree.

"Now that we know the purpose of the letter *a* we will learn how to pronounce the letter *b*," continued Cox.

By recess time, the entire class had learned how to read, and write, and pronounce the first five letters. While they were playing tag, Sally stuck out her tongue at Tom. "Well, Mr. Smart-alec, how does it feel to have the biggest feet in the county and be compared to the President of the United States?"

"It feels mighty fine."

"Well, I wouldn't feel so good if I were you. My pa told me that you're going to school on charity!"

"Charity? What's that?" Tom's eyes fell.

"Well, President Jackson, it means that someone else has to pay your tuition—all three cents a day of it."

Tom gulped. With effort, he managed to get back to his place on the split log without wiping his eyes.

During the rest of the class, Tom could not wait until the session was over.

That evening, while nibbling at a wedge of blueberry pie, Tom said, "Uncle Cummins, I sometimes get so discouraged I don't know what to do. It's terrible to be an orphan."

Cummins smiled. "Bein' an orphan has some disadvantages. But an orphan also has some advantages."

"Like?" Tom looked doubtful.

"Well, Old Hickory was an orphan; and that's what made him tough. He had to learn to stand on his own two feet from the time he was a youngun'. The other day while I was clearin' trees from the Keith place, I noticed that the trees that grew together were tall and straight. But those that had faced the winds by themselves, were far more rugged and a lot stronger. Now you're a-doin' all right. Colonel Talbott told me how he tested you by offerin' you a dollar and a quarter for that fish. You should be happy about the way you've learned to keep your word. A lot of people have never learned how to do that. A man who keeps his word is a powerful man, for people will trust him. Never forget that."

After three weeks of school, Tom was so discouraged he had to force himself to attend. On a Friday morning at breakfast, he said, "Uncle Cummins, I feel like dropping out."

"Oh, you can't be a quitter. Jacksons don't quit!" He spread some applesauce on a thick slice of toast. "Did I ever tell you about the first Jackson in our family who came to America?"

Tom leaned forward eagerly. "You never did," he replied, his blue eyes brightening.

"Wal, as far as I can figger, John Jackson—he's the one who grew up in the same county in which Old

Hickory grew up—left England in 1748. That was a
long time ago. He started workin' on the plantations
of Lord Baltimore in Maryland.

"Old John, like most of the other Jacksons, soon
got tired of workin' for someone else. And so he and
his wife Elizabeth moved to a place on the south
branch of the Potomac.

"Later, he and Liz moved again. This time they
crossed the Allegheny Ridge and built a home on the
Buckhannon River.

"Them days, Tom, was hard. Injuns was
everywhere. John and Liz had to build a stockade,
and they marked out their land with a tomahawk.
John was so tough, the neighbors called his place
Jackson's Fort." He laughed. "Keep your shoulders
up, Tom. Your ma told you that you should amount
to somethin' and I believe you will. Deed I do."

Shoulders back, chin thrust forward, Tom marched
off to school with new confidence. But his confidence
didn't last. He still remained at the bottom. Then on
a Monday afternoon, Teacher Cox asked him to
remain after school.

"Tom, I believe in you," said the bald man. "And
I believe that you'll amount to something. Right now
you're a slow learner. But don't let that discourage
you. Mushrooms grow overnight, and yet they don't
last. Yesterday, I found something that will help you.
It's called *Dilworth's Spelling-Book*. It's an old, old book.
Was first published in England but this is a new
American edition." He handed Tom a worn copy.

"Now I'm not giving you this book, I'm merely
lending it to you. Books like these are as scarce as hen's
teeth."

Tom's eyes widened as he held it in his own hands.
"I do thank you Mr. Cox. But I have a problem—"
He bit his lip.

"Yes?"

"Uncle Cummins has bought some new land and he wants me to oversee the slaves while they clear it. I have to keep them working until sundown, and then it's dark."

"Mmmm. You do have a problem." The teacher massaged his bald head as he pondered. Then he brightened. "But, Tom, you're a Jackson. Jacksons can do almost anything. You'll think of something. This book is a gold mine of knowledge, and it's especially good for beginners. Just look at this, it not only shows the sound of each letter, but it also has a paragraph made up of only three-letter words."

Pointing to several sentences, the teacher said: "Listen, Tom, while I read them. Notice that not one of the words has more than three letters. Are you ready?"

Tom nodded.

Touching each separate word, the teacher read:

> *"No man may put off the law of God."*
> *"The way of God is no ill way ."*
> *"My joy is in God all the day."*
> *"A bad man is a foe to God."*

Tom watched and listened eagerly. Then he exclaimed, "Mr. Cox, there is one word in those sentences that I already know."

"Which one?"

"I know the word *is*, and it's used three times!" His face split into a grin. "Oh, this is wonderful. Wonderful. Wonderful." He shook his head in amazement.

"You're doing well," assured Cox. "Now, after you've learned to read three-letter words, you can study some longer ones. Here, for example, is a prayer you probably learned from your mother. The words in it are very short. Only two of them have as many

as six letters. Listen as I point to the words and read
them.''

Enunciating carefully, the teacher read:

> *Now I lay me down to sleep*
> *I pray the Lord my soul to keep;*
> *If I should die before I wake,*
> *I pray the Lord my soul to take.*

Tom's eyes glistened. ''Thank you, Mr. Cox.
Thank you, thank you!'' he exclaimed. ''I'm going
to study so hard I'll soon be at the top of the class.''

Eagerly Tom headed home, sat on his bed, and
began to study the Dilworth speller. Each of the words
was a challenge. Soon he was able to read the words:
is, *no*, *all*, *of*, and *a*. He was just beginning to glance
at the prayer which he had learned from his mother,
and which he already knew by heart, when his uncle
appeared in the doorway.''

''I see you have a book,'' he said.

Tom explained how the teacher had loaned it to
him and how he was going to study it on his own.

''It's very interesting,'' said Cummins agreeably.
''But I have a job for you. The new bull has broken
down the fence, and I want you to go with me and
watch as the workers repair it.''

''Now?'' Tom's eyes fell.

''Yes, right now. It'll soon be dark.''

''But I wanted to study the book!''

''Studying books *is* important. But learning how
to repair a fence is *also* important.''

Reluctantly, Tom hid the book under the bed and
followed his uncle.

4

The Boy Who Refused To Stop Learning

Accompanying his uncle, Tom followed him over to the row of shacks where the slaves lived. After knocking at a door, Cummins half-shouted, "Uncle Robinson, the new bull has broken the fence. Round up some men. Let's repair it."

"Yes, Massa, I'll be right wid you."

Soon three or four slaves, together with Uncle Robinson's son Jim who was about the age of Tom, were standing outside.

"Hate to ruin your suppers," said Cummins as the smell of fried onions filled the air. "But we don't want him to go a-rovin' round da country. I managed to get him into the corral, but we shouldn't keep him there. He deserves *some* freedom."

Skillfully, Uncle Robinson and his friends worked on the fence. But more of it had to be repaired than any of them had figured. Soon it was dark.

"Massa, maybe we should finish it tomorrow,"

suggested Robinson as he nailed a section of barbed wire into place. "It's 'most too dark to work."

"I know you're hungry. But we'd better finish it now. Jim, you and Tom get a pine knot."

As Jim held the blazing torch, the men completed the repairs and then returned to their shacks. Tom washed his face at the pump and took his place at the table in the big house. "I'm sorry the food is a leetle cold," apologized Aunt Robinson. She retied the apron that squeezed her ample waist. "It's gettin' late. Was spectin' you more den three hours ago. It's hard to keep food hot. Deed it am."

"Never mind, you're the best cook in the country," assured Cummins as he greedily heaped his plate with fried potatoes smothered in onions, and selected a large pork chop. "Just the other day a man offered me fifteen hundred dollars for you. I told him you weren't for sale at any price."

"Thank you, Massa. I does my best," she replied over her shoulder as she retreated into the kitchen.

Tom wolfed the food down as fast as possible. His mind was on that spelling book.

"What's the hurry?" asked his uncle.

"I want to study that book."

After he had gulped down the last bite, Tom hurried into his room. With only the stump of a candle for light, he started at the very beginning of the book. He observed each letter and then searched for that identical letter in each of the three-letter words in the easy sentences. Soon he was reading entire words. When baffled, he studied the prayer which began "Now I lay me down to sleep." Knowing the words from memory, he was able to figure out the sounds of each new letter. Soon he was able to read entire sentences of the three-letter words.

Shortly, however, the flame in the stubby candle

fluttered and went out and he was forced to give up.

The next morning he hurried off to school with the widest steps he had ever taken. *Yes the world was wonderful!* At the end of the month he was near the top of the class. His best subject was arithmetic.

Tom attended this school for only forty-eight days. His share of the $1.39 tuition came from the trustees for the poor children. Later he attended several other schools for shorter periods. When Tom was fifteen, Colonel Withers announced that he would be teaching school in the Courthouse at Weston, a little town three or four miles south of Jackson's Mill.

Colonel Withers cut an unusual figure in this "western community." He wore a tall silk hat, quoted Latin and Greek—and had written a book, *The Chronicles of Border Warfare.*

Upon learning of the school, Tom enrolled immediately. Those who knew him agreed that his learning capacity was quite limited. In fact, Cummins thought Tom was the dullest of the Jonathan Jackson children and as a consequence, he received less education than Warren or Laura.

Tom relished Withers' teaching; but soon the man in the tall hat tired of the classroom, closed the school, and turned to other occupations. And yet Tom refused to stop learning. *If there was no school for him to attend he would teach himself!* But where would he find the time after supervising the slaves? While pondering his problem, he suddenly bumped into a solution.

As he walked home with Jim, he said, "I have a new job for you."

"Yes, Little Massa?"

"I want you to hold a burning pine knot over me each night while I read."

"Don't you have candles?"

"I do but a pine knot will make more light."

"And where you all want me to do this?"

"Oh, maybe in the barn or under a tree."

"Little Massa, sometimes you amazes me. Every time you have an extra moment you stick your nose in da Bible. Why do you like to read so much?"

"I'll tell you, Jim, why I like to read. I like to read because my ma told me that I should really amount to something. Uncle Cummins told me that I may be related to President Jackson himself."

Jim sighed. "I wish I could read. But the slaveholders don't want their slaves to learn nothin'."

"Don't worry, Jim. Tell you what I'll do. Each evening after you've held the pine knot over my head while I learn, I'll teach you to read."

"Really?" Jim's eyes widened.

"Yes, really."

"Won't dat get yous into trouble?"

"Naw. We won't tell anyone."

"When do we start?"

"Tonight!"

After supper, Tom met Jim in an empty shack. "I'm going to start reading my Bible," announced Tom. He opened it to the first chapter.

After an hour had passed and he had finally stumbled through the entire chapter, Tom taught Jim how to recognize and pronounce the first five letters of the alphabet. Three weeks later Jim also made his way through the first chapter of Genesis.

"This makes me very happy," exulted Jim. "Our preacher can't even read one word. Soon I'll be able to read to him." He laughed. "Maybe if'n I do dat we'll hear a new sermon. Am gettin'plumb tired of hearin' 'bout Jonah and dat big fish."

They both laughed.

One day while riding in a buggy with his uncle,

Tom had a question. "Why is it that the slaveholders don't want their slaves to learn to read?"

"Because if they learn to read they'll quit workin'."

"But *you* work all the time and *you* know how to read."

"Yes, I know. Nevertheless, when slaves learn to read they get unhappy."

"Why?"

Cummins shrugged. "Because those who learn to read know too much for their own good."

"Like what?"

"Like escaping to Canada and being freed."

"How could that be?"

"Because all the slaves in the British Empire were freed in 1833, and Canada is a part of the British Empire."

Tom frowned. "Canada is a long way from here. How could a penniless slave get to Canada?"

"By the underground railway."

"Underground railway? What's that?"

"Up north there are people who so hate slavery they hide the slaves in their basements or perhaps in their barns or even in haystacks. Then, when it's dark, they put 'em in a wagon, cover 'em with straw, and take 'em to the next place on the underground railway. After that, the next man does the same. It takes months for them to get to Canada."

"Have you ever had any slaves escape on the underground railway?"

"Never! And the reason's simple. I treat my slaves right. Each has a garden. I provide their clothes, let 'em go to church—and I never breaks up families. All of 'em are my friends. The Robinsons would give their lives for me."

"Does Jim belong to you?"

"Shore does."

"But you didn't buy him!"

"No, but I bought his parents. Bought 'em at an auction. Paid nine hundred for his mother and a thousand for his father. Jim belongs to me just as that colt over there belong to me." He pointed. "He belongs to me because I own the stallion and the mare that produced him."

"Do you think it's right to own a human being?"

"The laws of Virginia say so, and I follow the law!"

While shuffling this around in his mind, Tom focused his eyes on a nearby herd of cattle. Eventually, he said, "Uncle Cummins, if most people in the North hate slavery, and most people in the South believe in slavery, how can these two sections of people get along?"

"You've asked a tough question. I'm afraid they won't. Someday there'll be war between the North and the South. It will be a terrible war. Brothers will fight brothers."

"Why?"

"Because there are slave holders in the North, and there are those who hate slavery in the South."

"Then we'll have bloody days ahead?" Tom shuddered.

"Yes, we're in for a blood bath—a dreadful blood bath."

When Tom was twelve, his brother Warren, who had left because of his uncle's restraints, showed up.

"Where've you been?" demanded Tom as he grabbed his hand and pulled him through the door.

"I've been teachin' school."

"Do you like it?"

"Of course. Each of my little scholars pays three cents a day. That adds up. But I have a new idea and I need your help."

"What is it?"

"I better not tell you until I get a good night's sleep."

"Why not?"

"It may chill your blood. Besides, I want to talk to Uncle Cummins about it first. I'd hate to get his dander up."

When Cummins returned that afternoon he was so excited to see Warren, he rushed into the kitchen. "Aunt Robinson," he almost shouted, "Warren's here. Cook somethin' special."

"Yes, Massa Cummins, I'll do dat." She thoughtfully licked her lips and retied her apron. "As I 'members, he specially likes chitlins and fried taters. Yeah, dat's what I'll cook."

"And add some onions," put in Tom. "The smell of cookin' onions will make him as hungry as a b'ar."

"Sho 'nuff." She laughed and returned to the kitchen.

Following a huge breakfast of ham and eggs and grits, Warren said, "Let's go for a walk so I can let you in on my plans."

After they had passed the slave quarters, Warren said, "Now I'll clue you in as to what I have in mind. It's kinda scary."

Tom tossed away a branch lying across the path. "I'm listening."

"We'll go over to Uncle Neale's in Ohio where I've been staying—"

"What's scary about that?"

"The Neales own a small island on the Ohio River. It's covered with trees. They make lots of money selling firewood to the steamboat captains who pass by."

"So?" Tom cleared another branch from the path.

"So we'll help them, and learn the business. Then,

we'll move onto another island, and do the same. We'll get rich.''

''Just any island?''

''No, we'll find an island were no one lives—and claim it.''

''And where will we live?''

Warren shrugged. ''Oh, we'll build a shack.''

''Out of what?''

''Sticks and leaves and mud, and—''

''And where will we cook?''

''Outside between three stones.''

''Like the Indians?''

''Sure. Why not?''

''And what will we eat?''

''We'll catch fish and snare a few rabbits.''

Tom stared. Then he laughed. ''Your idea is more than scary. It's plumb crazy! But you're three years older than I am. Tell you what. If Uncle Cummins agrees, I'll give it a try.''

''Then shake on it.''

They shook hands with great solemnity. Then they laughed.

5

A New Adventure

Tom's heart thumped like a drum while Warren explained their plans to his uncle. "After we've spent a week or two with the Neales on their little island," he said, "we'll find an island of our own. Then we'll start cutting wood for the steamboats. What do you think of that?"

Instead of answering, Cummins reached for another fried egg.

"Uncle Cummins, is that a good idea?" Warren smiled.

Again, Cummins remained silent.

"If the captains don't stop at our island, we'll move to another," continued Warren, urging a comment.

Acting as if he had not heard, Cummins continued to chew, swallow, and reach for more food.

"Between the two of us, we'll make a lot of money," he added. "Do you have any suggestions?"

Silence.

"We'll have a lot of fun," put in Tom with a nervous laugh.

Silence.

"Maybe we'll earn enough money to buy a little farm," suggested Warren.

Cummins stared, but although his jaws continued up and down, his lips remained as silent as a slit in a pumpkin.

The boys exchanged glances. Then Tom said, "Uncle, you're a lot older than us. We need advice."

Suddenly the grim pumpkin slit twisted into a smile, and then it expanded into a laugh. "Boys," said Cummins, "both of you remind me of that prize bull that tore down my fence."

Tom's heart sank. "In what way?" he asked.

"That bull cost me a lot of money, even more than a slave. And do you know why he cost me so much money?"

"Why?" asked the boys almost together.

"Because he has good rich blood! And both of you have good rich blood." He paused to swat a fly that was scrubbing its face on his bald spot. "You boys are full of Jackson blood, the same blood that has flowed—and still flows—in the veins of some of the finest men in America. Never forget that Old Hickory is a Jackson!" The fly returned and perched on the end of his nose. After he brushed it away, he concluded, "Your idea is a daring one. I hope you succeed. But even if you don't you'll have a fine experience. Great lives are built on failures. When you get tired of the river, you can return here. I'll always have somethin' for you to do."

After two weeks with the Neales, and after they had learned how to chop down a tree so that it would fall in the right direction, the boys borrowed a boat and prepared to discover their own private island.

The adventurers were stepping into the boat when Mrs. Neales rushed up. "What are you going to eat?" she demanded.

"Fish and rabbits, and maybe some berries," replied Warren.

"Are you going to eat them raw?" Her eyes bulged.

"Of course not."

"Well, here's a frying pan and some salt and pepper and some knives and forks. And just in case you get hungry before you've set up housekeeping, here's a loaf of bread and a bit of ham."

The sun was near the horizon before the boys discovered an ideal spot to start their business. After landing, they constructed a put-together shelter made of limbs. Next, they began to explore the island. "There are plenty of trees," commented Tom, slapping a slender one with his hand.

"Yes, but the live ones won't do. They're too green to burn. What we must do is find dead ones and chop them into the right lengths," explained Warren. He spoke with authority.

Tired from hours of rowing, Tom eventually built a fire near the shelter, and fried a slab of ham.

Holding a ham sandwich in his hands, Warren started to take a bite.

"Stop!" exclaimed Tom.

"What's the matter?"

"We haven't thanked the Lord for our food."

Warren stared. "The Neales never pray before they eat."

"Uncle Cummins doesn't either. But Ma taught me to pray. She told me that even a pig says *oink oink* before it eats, and that we're better than pigs! And even though Uncle Cummins never prayed nor went to church, I prayed silently before each meal. I still pray before I go to bed."

While darkness was settling over the island a large steamboat came churning by. "Look at that!"

exclaimed Tom. ''And look at all the black smoke swirlin' out the chimbleys. It must take a lot of firewood to keep those forty-foot wheels a-turnin'. Warren, we'll have to chop a lot of wood!''

Tom was so excited, he found it hard to get to sleep. As he twisted on the slender mattress he had brought, he thought about what he was going to do with all the money he would be earning. The first one who would benefit, he decided, would be Laura Ann.

He was on the verge of slipping into unconsciousness when a cloud of mosquitoes swished through the front opening of the shed. Uttering war cries as they hovered around him, searching for choice places to drill, they went to work. Soon he was slapping with both hands. Then he began to slap and shout at the same time. ''Take that, and that, and that,'' he cried. The mosquitoes paid little attention to his slaps and cries. They loved his type of blood and were determined to have their fill.

His face swollen from their deadly work, Tom leaped out of bed and went to the stones where the fire had been. Hurriedly, he lit another. Perhaps the smoke would help! As he struggled to get it going, Warren emerged. By the light of the stars, Tom noticed that Warren's face was also swollen.

"We should have brought some mosquito nets," grumbled Tom as he felt the lumps all over his face and arms.

Warren shrugged. "Oh, we'll be all right. A few mosquito bites never killed anyone."

Presently a fire was crackling. The heat and smoke drove the mosquitoes away, but it soon became so hot the boys were forced into their shelter. Struggling to subdue the singing pests which had now returned with reinforcements, and also keep the fire going, Tom prayed that daylight would hurry up and come.

After what seemed an eternity, beams of sunlight gradually lit the river.

Following a breakfast of ham and bread, Warren reached for an ax. "We'd better get started," he announced. "We can't sell firewood if we don't have a big stack of it."

Working together, the boys assembled a huge pile of dead wood in front of their shelter. They had just finished it when a huge steamboat came churning down the river.

"This is our chance!" yelled Warren. "When it gets near, yell and point at our firewood."

"How much should we charge for the wood?" asked Tom.

"Leave that to me, but prepare to yell," replied Warren.

Tom almost held his breath until the prow of the steamer was just a few lengths north of them. Then

he funneled his hands and yelled, "Firewood!
Firewood!" But the man behind the wheel, whom he
could see clearly, didn't even glance in their direction.

After three more similar experiences, Warren said,
"Maybe they don't see us. Tom, you climb up in that
tree over there and wave that old flag we brought."

As Tom sat in the highest crotch in the tree, dozens
of ants began to chew on him. He was about to
descend when he noticed another two-wheeler
approaching. Bracing himself so that he could wave
the flag and not fall, he waited until the boat was in
correct position. This time it seemed to be less than
two hundred yards away.

"All right, yell and wave the flag," ordered
Warren.

Tom followed orders, but was again ignored.

"M-maybe it's because they don't see the wood,"
suggested Warren. "Lets stack it on the water's
edge."

Two hours later, after the wood had been stacked,
Tom shinnied up the tree again. Then he shouted,
"Wow! A big one's on the way, and it's crammed
with passengers."

Soon the *Marybelle* came puffing along. It was much
closer than any of the other steamboats had been. As
Tom waited, he suddenly shouted, "Toot! Toot! The
big one's a-comin'!"

"Then shout and keep shouting," screamed
Warren.

Tom waved the flag and shouted, and some of the
passengers waved back. But the *Marybelle's* mighty
wheels continued to turn as it kept moving south.
Suddenly Warren began to jump up and down.

"What's the matter?" exclaimed Tom

"Look! Look!" he cried. "The backlash of the boat
has washed most of our firewood into the river."

"Our time's been wasted!" grumbled Tom. "What's next?"

"All I know is that I'm hungry," replied Warren.

"Would you like a ham sandwich?" Tom forced a smile.

"No! All we've had to eat on this trip is ham. We've had ham for breakfast, lunch and supper. Let's have some fried eggs for a change."

"But we don't have any eggs and I don't have any money."

"Never mind, I have seven dollars. We'll row over to a store and get some."

The storekeeper eyed them suspiciously. "And so you want a dozen eggs and a yard of mosquito netting. That's a real combination! How ya all gonna cook it?" He squirted a stream of tobacco juice into the spittoon near his feet.

Warren explained what they were doing and the curious lines on the man's face softened. "Wal," he said, screwing his walrus moustache to an angle with a twist of his lips, "you ain't a-gonna sell no firewood to these captains in this neck of the woods. Now if I was you, I'd head for the Mississippi. There's plenty of money down there."

The boys were ready to leave when the storekeeper held up his hand. "Ain't you gonna buy no bread? If you have eggs you need bread."

"Oh, thank you," replied Warren laying a nickel on the counter.

While rowing over to the island, the boys agreed to take the gentleman's advice. After a quick breakfast, they headed south and then west on the broad Ohio. Each day they went as far as possible, stopped at little towns for groceries, and then traveled on. While hugging the north side of the river, they passed a little Ohio town called "Ripley." Perched on a high cliff at this place, Tom noticed a brick house with deeply worn paths leading up to it. He was curious because of the sheerness of the cliff and the firmness of the paths.

"Look, Warren," he said while pointing. "Why would anyone want to climb such a steep path?"

Warren shook his head. "I don't know," he replied.

"Well, I'm going to find out. It mystifies me."

The next day when they stopped on the opposite side of the river, Tom approached the grocer. "Why would anyone want to have a house perched on a cliff like that?" he asked.

"Oh," replied the slender man who sported a full beard, "that's probably the home of John Rankin. He's an abolitionist."

"And what's an abolitionist?"

"They're determined people who want to put an end to slavery immediately."

"And what does Rankin do?"

"He keeps a light burning in front of his house to attract the slaves who've crossed the river. Then he feeds 'em and takes 'em to the next place on the underground railway. He's a Presbyterian preacher and as determined as sin. The rascal helped three of my slaves escape." He pulled his beard.

"But the Ohio is at least half a mile wide. How do they cross?" Tom stared out the window at the huge body of water.

"Some have boats. One gal crossed by leapin' from one cake of ice to another. And she did it with a little boy in her arms." He shook his head. "Her name was Eliza."

"Since Kentucky is a slave state and Ohio is a free state, do you think we'll have a war?" persisted Tom.

"I'm afraid so."

Eventually the boys found a choice island on the

Mississippi close to the southwestern Kentucky border. This new base of operations even had the remants of an old cabin which they fixed up and made mosquito-proof. The island was littered with logs that had washed ashore—and with numerous dead trees.

After surveying the island, Tom said, "This is the place! The good Lord has answered my prayers."

"Let's hope some boats stop," cautioned Warren.

After three days of hard work, and after the boys had prepared a huge pile of firewood, a small steamboat dropped anchor nearby, and sent over some men to negotiate with them. They bought all of their wood, and promised to return. Tom gulped as the leader counted out the money.

The next day another boat stopped and then another and another. At last they were making money. In addition, Tom caught enough fish to keep their stomachs full.

But after several weeks, each began to have aches and chills and develop a fever. Yet they forced themselves to keep their axes swinging. Then Warren acquired a cough that wouldn't stop.

Finally, after they had been away from Virginia for three months, the boys decided that it was time for them to return to Uncle Cummins' place. "But we can't go empty-handed," objected Tom. "We *should* have something to show for all of our work."

Warren agreed, so they rowed over to a little town and each purchased a new trunk. Then, with a little money still remaining in their pockets, they lifted their anchor and started home.

Uncle Cummins was glad to see them.

6

From Teacher To Constable

Now that they were not traveling, the boys had no need for their trunks, so Warren gave his to his half brother Wirt Woodson, and Tom presented his to Laura who still lived with the Neales in Ohio.

Tom's health improved each day; but Warren's worsened. After a violent fit of coughing, he noticed a crimson spot in his handkershief. *Could it be that he was a victim* of that dreaded lung disease called *consumption*? The thought shattered him, for there was no cure for *consumption*—as tuberculosis was then called. It often wiped out entire families. Refusing to expose Tom, Warren moved back to Buckhannon County where he had taught school.

With both Warren and Laura gone, Tom was the only member of Jonathan Jackson's family who remained with Uncle Cummins. Tom kept busy supervising the slaves.

Several months after his return from the Mississippi, Cummins approached after a grueling day spent
clearing trees. "Tom," he said, "Major Minton
Bailey from Weston asked if you'd like to work for
him."

"Doing what?" Tom cocked his head to one side.

"He's responsible for issuing contracts on the new
Staunton-Parkersburg turnpike."

"In Lewis County?"

"That's right. He heard that you're good with
figures, and so—"

"You mean that I might help survey?" Tom's eyes
glistened.

"I don't know about that, but—"

"George Washington was a surveyor!" exlaimed
Tom. "Oh, I hope I can get that job. It would change
my life."

"The job is yours, but I can't promise that you'll
became a surveyor." Cummins laughed.

Although Tom went to work on the turnpike, there
is no record that he became a surveyor. But
undoubtedly, he learned the basic techniques of the
profession. The work was hard; and being away from
Warren and Laura was discouraging. Concerned by
his despair, a worker made a suggestion: "There's
a Methodist church three miles from here. Why don't
you start attending their services?"

Tom liked the idea. Feeling that maybe God could
help him, Tom made the six-mile trip by foot each
Sunday. Although the sermons were long the services
inspired him to spend more time with his Bible.

After he had finished his assignment on the
turnpike, he returned to his Uncle's home. While
awaiting another job, a friend by the name of Joe
Lightburn became fascinated at the way Tom read
the Bible. Soon, they began to explore it together.

Anxious to continue one of the chapters, Joe borrowed Tom's copy. In return, he loaned Tom his copy of Parson Weems' *Life of General Francis Marion.*

Sitting on a bench beneath the cool shade of a tree, Tom opened the tattered book and began to read. Soon he was spellbound, for Weems knew how to hold a reader's interest. The opening lines were breathtaking:

> *One thousand seven hundred and thirty-two was a glorious year for America. It gave birth to two of the noblest thunderbolts of her wars, George Washington and Francis Marion. The latter was born in St. John's Parish, South Carolina. His father also was a Carolinian, but his grandfather was a Huguenot or French Protestant, who lived near Rochelle in the blind and bigoted days of Louis XIV.*

The story of Marion, the Swamp Fox, gripped Tom. Marion's exploits became his exploits, and Marion's narrow escapes became Tom's narrow escapes. Tom even read between the lines.

He especially liked "Marion's brigade." Those volunteers owned their own horses, and were ready to leap into the saddle the instant they were needed. Although frequently hungry, they were as loyal to Marion as the Apostle John had been to Jesus.

While reading the book and tingling at every event, Tom had an opportunity to open a school. He was only sixteen, and didn't have any kind of diploma. Still, he was the most qualified candidate in the area, and so he was hired. "The tuition will be yours," explained the one in charge of the "Literary Fund."

Since there was no glass in any of the "windows," Tom covered the empty spaces with oiled paper. Five rows of split logs formed the seats, and his desk was a short up-ended log just as it had been in each of the schools he had attended.

Tom's knees wobbled when he faced the five twelve-year-olds who made up his entire class. He remembered the terror he had endured the first time he shaved. He had borrowed his uncle's razor, and his uncle had warned. "Now don't cut off your ears!"

After lathering each place where whiskers had sprouted, he slowly, ever so slowly, began to scrape. As he scraped, he knew that the straight-edge had to be held at just the right angle. If he slanted it too much, he might cut himself; and if he didn't slant it enough, the long steel blade would merely bend the whiskers without cutting them. Also, while scraping, if he accidentally pulled the blade lengthwise, he would cut himself. That first shaving ordeal had lasted half an hour and he had only nicked himself three times!

Strangely, memories of that ordeal, made him realize, as he stood before his class that he would have to overcome his fears, and do the very best be could. And so, ignoring the expanding hollow place in his stomach, he forced himself over to the blackboard and wrote:

A man of words and not of deeds
Is like a garden full of weeds

"Those words," he said, making an effort to keep a quiver out of his voice, "state the motto of my life. And I hope they will become the motto of your lives. All of us can learn from the chickens. Many people cluck even though they haven't accomplished anything. A hen never does that! A hen only clucks after she's laid an egg."

When the laughter quieted, Tom registered the names of all five of the pupils in his notebook, but he was secretly worried about how he could teach them.

Suddenly Martha, a plump girl on the front log, raised her hand. "Mr. Jackson," she inquired, "are you sick?"

"No. Why do you ask?"

"Because your face is drippin'. . ."

Tom touched his cheek, and it was sopping wet.

Ignoring the question, he asked, "How many of you know how to read?" Since none of them did, he relaxed for he'd had the experience of teaching Jim to read and knew just what to do. Feeling better, he wrote the first five letters of the alphabet on the blackboard, and taught them the way he had been taught.

"Soon you'll all be able to read the motto, I wrote when we started this morning," he said. After a long day, it was time to ring the dismissal bell.

Each day of teaching seemed to leave Tom drained. This meant that if he were to continue teaching, he'd have to cram his head full of additional knowledge. Going from door to door, he borrowed every book in the neighborhood. Then he kept a series of candles burning late while he studied the books and made notes.

As he studied and taught, he developed an intense hunger to go to college. This, of course, was an impossibility; for he was many miles from the nearest college—and he had no money.

Tom had just finished his second semester of teaching when his Uncle Cummins approached. "You're a good teacher," he remarked a little sarcastically.

"Who told you that?" asked Tom, beaming.

"No one," he replied crisply. "Jim ran off, and I've been told that the reason he managed to get away is because you taught him to read. Did you?" He scowled and rubbed his bald spot.

"Yes, Uncle Cummins, I did."

Cummins snorted. "Jim was a good worker. Could have sold him for at least five hundred dollars."

Tom stared at the ground.

"Never mind. Knowledge is power. Let's hope Jim does well in Canada." Suddenly, his uncle's mood changed. "Tom," he asked, "How'd you like to be a constable?"

"A constable? I'm only seventeen!"

"That doesn't matter. Colonel Withers and Major Baily would like for you to be a constable."

Tom brightened. "Sounds exciting. I'm ready. But I'll never be elected." He laughed.

"We'll find out next month," replied Cummins, "and while we're waiting you can get Uncle Robinson and some of the other slaves to repair the fence. That bull has ripped another hole right in the middle of it."

It was hard for Tom to keep his mind on the fence. Finally it was June 8, 1841, when nominations would be made. Both Tom and Robert Hall were nominated, and it was announced that the deciding votes would be cast three days later. Tom found it harder than ever before to wait out those three days.

As he waited, he wrote down the names of those who were authorized to vote. At times he thought he'd win; at other times he was certain that he would lose.

Eventually the three long summer days passed and the votes were cast. The Colonel and Major and three of their friends voted for Tom, but a whopping twelve voted for Robert Hall. Tom was keenly disappointed. But then, on that same day, a mysterious event took place—an event no historian has been able to explain. Perhaps because Hall was unable to accept the position, the county court appointed *five* constables.

Tom Jackson was one of the five!

At the appointed time, the legal statement concerning Tom's new position, was printed and posted in the courthouse. The bulletin board, read:

Thomas Jackson who was appointed constable in the 2nd district in this county this day appeared in open court and entered into bond with security in the penalty of $2,000 which bond is duly recorded, and took the several oaths prescribed by law, the court being of the opinion that he is man of honesty, probity and good demeanor.

Tom studied every bulletin he could find which outlined the kind of work he was to do. Since his former teacher, Colonel Withers, and his friend Major Bailey were justices of the peace they coached him.

"You will be required to serve papers, collect judgments, and act as an agent for the justices," instructed Withers. "Some of the people you will face will be tough. Many will try to frighten you— especially if you're out to collect a judgment. Remember that you're a Jackson! That means: never retreat."

After a few weeks of duty, Tom was trapped in a nearly impossible situation. An extremely difficult gentleman owed money to a needy widow, and he vowed that he would never pay it. Tom was assigned to this task, so he went to Colonel Withers to ask his advice.

"Lasso his horse and bring it in. But remember, Tom, it's against the law to capture a horse if the owner is on it. That means that you'll have to figure out a way to catch the horse when it's alone." He laughed. "You have a tough assignment. It will prove whether or not you're a *real* Jackson."

By a little detective work, Tom identified the livery stable where the debtor kept his horse. Biding his time, he waited until the owner rode up and dismounted. Then he seized it by the reins. The owner responded by leaping back into the saddle. "Now, you dirty, lowdown duck-footed brat, you'd better let me go.

You know the law!'' He squirted a stream of amber juice.

Tom had an idea. Refusing to release the reins he led the astonished horse into a stable that was so low the rider had to dismount or be crushed by the top of the entrance. Livid with anger and shouting oaths, the scoundrel lashed the horse with his whip. Nonetheless, Tom quickly pulled the horse outside and led it to the courthouse. There, amidst the cheers of onlookers, it was duly secured.

Tom was the hero of the day. ''You're a *real* Jackson,'' assured Withers, slapping him on the shoulder.

7

Bolted Doors

Tom enjoyed his work as constable. It was fun to outwit those who tried to avoid being served papers, or who sought to escape paying judgments decreed by the court. But he also enjoyed the steady income.

All was well with him until he received word that Warren was near death and would like for him and Laura Ann to pay a final visit.

That November, 1841, Tom and Laura stood at Warren's bedside. Consumption had wasted his body until he was little more than a skeleton. He and Tom reviewed the exciting things they had done together—especially their jaunt down the Mississippi. But within days Warren was seized by a bit of coughing and began to hemorrhage. Soon he was gone.

"Just think, Laura," observed Tom, "he was only twenty, and now we're the only ones left in the family. If we're to make our lives count, we'll have to hurry." His smile was grim.

Tom later wrote to his Uncle Neale, "My brother died in the hope of a bright immortality at the right hand of his Redeemer."

Warren's premature death and the way he was loved by those near him, had a profound effect on both Tom and Laura, and others too. In his honor, county authorities gave the district where he had lived the name of Warren.

While Tom was still a constable, Cummins asked him to go to Parkersburg and bring home a piece of machinery for the mill which was being shipped there from Pittsburgh. Since this journey would take several days, Tom asked Thaddeus Moore to accompany him.

The pair spent Sunday in Weston and went to hear Mr. Quillin, a Presbyterian, preach. Tom was so impressed by his morning sermon, he insisted on returning at early candle light to hear him again. On their way back, Tom said, "I like Presbyterian doctrine. It suits me just right."

Before continuing on their journey, Tom arranged for them to stop at Clarksburg. "I want to visit the home where I was born," he explained. After viewing the three-room brick house, Tom led Moore into the backyard. Pointing to an apple tree, he said, "That tree was planted by Johnny Appleseed." He put his hand on the trunk. "His real name is John Chapman. God assigned him the task of planting apples, and he's been so faithful we now call him Johnny Appleseed. He really made his life count. Even after he's gone, many of his trees will remain. I, also, want to make my life count. Now let's go over to the cemetery. I want to see where my father is buried."

Tom searched through the graveyard, but even though he asked the caretaker for help, he was unable to find the grave. "They were utterly destitute when he died, and they couldn't afford a marker. I don't remember much about Pa," he murmured. "But Ma assured me that he was a good man. She's the one

I remember; and although her grave was not marked her last words have blossomed in my heart." He wiped his eyes and blew his nose.

"What were they?"

"She said—" He struggled with his tears. "She said, 'The secret of living right is to stay close to the Lord. You must learn to pray. Pray when you go to bed. Pray when you get up. Pray during the day. And have faith.' "

After they left the graveyard, they rode for at least half an hour in complete silence. Then after making a turn in the road, Tom remarked, "Thad, I've tried to follow her wishes. I do, yes, I do want to make my life count for something."

A little later, Tom continued, "For some unknown reason Ma gave only my sister Laura two names. She's Laura Ann. Warren and I are stuck with only one name."

"Oh, that doesn't make any difference," replied Thaddaeus.

"I guesss not. But I'd still like to have a middle name."

After Tom's statement, he remained silent again for a long time. Then he spoke with enthusiasm, "I know what I'll do. I'll add my father's name to my own. Yes, that's what I'll do! From now on my name is Thomas Jonathan Jackson."

One evening after they reached the Stone House at Pennsboro in western Virginia, they were greeted with the words, "You boys are in luck, Sam Houston, the president of the Republic of Texas is here! He'll be anxious to see you."

"Why? I've never met him." Tom frowned.

"Because he's from Rockbridge. As the crow flies, that's only a hundred miles south of Clarksburg."

"I know where that is." Tom's eyes brightened.

"I stopped there when I worked on the Staunton-Parkersburg turnpike."

Soon they were introduced.

Tom shook hands with the balding man who was wearing a dark tie and sideburns, and wondered what to say. But Houston broke the ice with one blow. "So you're a Jackson," he said. "Any relation to old Hickory?"

"Our distant relatives came from the same county in the Old Country," replied Tom, trying to be modest, but not succeeding very well.

"That's wonderful! I was in his army when we fought the Creeks. He was a great president. I learned a lot about him when I was governor of Tennessee. He helped frame their constitution, and has been given credit for giving the state its name."

"And now you're president of Texas. Right?"

"I'm the president of the *Republic* of Texas," corrected Houston. "Texas isn't yet a part of the Union."

Tom asked questions and learned much about Texans, especially their bravery when Mexicans attacked the Alamo. After a long conversation, Houston held out his hand. "I must leave. Have an appointment," he explained.

"One more question, President Houston," pled Tom.

"Speak. What's on your mind?"

"If you were my age, what would you do?"

"I'd go to college." After that remark, Houston picked up his hat and strode out of the room.

The next day, as the boys continued on their journey, Tom said, "President Houston suggested that I go to college. But Thad, how can I do that? I don't have any money."

"Maybe your uncle Cummins would help . . ."

"I don't think so. All his money's tied up in farms. He's even mortgaged some of his slaves."

"Then why don't you go to West Point? West Point's free."

"I never thought of that!" exclaimed Tom.

Toward noon the pair stopped to eat the lunch they had prepared at Pennsboro. After Tom prayed and while they were eating, their horses helped themselves to some nearby oats.

When they were ready to leave, Tom said, "Now let's go to the cabin and pay the lady for the oats."

"Are you serious?" Thad shook his head.

"Of course. The Bible says 'Thou shalt not steal.' "

Somewhat shocked, Thad followed Tom over to the cabin. When the lady refused to accept payment, Tom found a penny with a hole in it. "Take this," he said. "You can hang it around your baby's neck. He can use it to help cut his teeth."

Thad was a "diary keeper" and had been writing each day of the journey. That evening he picked up a pencil and wrote "Tom seems to have strong streak of honesty in him. . . . Anyway, he said that we need not be ashamed when we pass the house on our return."

Eventually, the boys got to Parkersburg, picked up the spare part, and headed back home. As they were riding along, Tom said, "You suggested that I go to West Point. How does a person manage to go there?"

"I had a friend who attended the academy for a year. He said it's really tough to get in."

"In what way?"

"Each student—they call 'em cadets—has to be nominated by a United States senator or congressman—or a territorial delegate if he lives in a territory. Also, he has to be between the age of seventeen and twenty-two."

"I'm of the right age," murmured Tom, thoughtfully, "Do—do you think I could find a member of Congress who would nominate me?"

"I don't know. But if I were you, I'd try. Those who graduate from West Point have it made. They start as second lieutenants in the regular army, and graduate with a B.S. degree."

After lunch, the boys remounted their horses. As they were passing Mr. Adams' farm, they noticed something going on. While they watched, workers brought a black coffin and laid it by a deep grave in the field. One of Mr Adam's slaves had died.

The sight prompted a discussion of slavery.

That night Thad confided to his diary: "Tom seemed to be very sorry for the slaves and thought they should be free and have a chance, and said that Joe Lightburn said they should be taught to read so they could read the Bible and he thought so too. I told him it would be better not to make known such views and if they were carried out we would have to black our own boots. He said with him that would only be on Sunday and not even in the winter."

Thad concluded his diary with the observation, "Tom is a first-rate boy and I am just getting to know him."

Tom kept thinking about his trip, especially Sam Houston. By searching the neighborhood, he found a book about the Alamo and was intrigued that Colonel William Barret Travis, the leader of the defenders of the church turned into a fort, was only twenty-six years, four months and twenty-five days old when the battle reached its climax.

Those figures meant that the now famous Travis had only been eight years older than himself! Pacing back and forth, he imagined himself leading a besieged

group of men surrounded by a vastly superior force
of screaming enemies. "Jack," he heard himself
shouting, "help us reload while we fire. We're
outnumbered ten to one, but we'll never surrender.
Never! . ."

Yes, he just *had* to go to West Point and become
an officer in the United States Army!

Ah, but how would a penniless orphan from the
hills like himself manage to be accepted into such
a distinguished place? He sighed and shook his head.
Like many of his other dreams this was an impossibility. But later in the day, he thought of others who
had achieved the impossible. President Jackson had
been an orphan. In his youth, Sam Houston had lived
with the Cherokee Indians for three years, and was
so much like them they adopted him into the tribe.
Also, he had very little education; and yet he was now
the president of the Republic of Texas! David Crockett
had not even learned to read until he was eighteen.
Nevertheless, he had become Congressman Crockett,
and had died a hero's death in the battle of the Alamo.

A few days later, while thinking about the
providence of God, Tom began to believe that a way
would eventually open for him to attend West Point.
And then he overheard that a cadet from his district
was needed at West Point.

Jumping grasshoppers, this was his opportunity!

Congressman Sam Hays who lived only a short
distance from Jackson's Mill, had befriended him.
Tom remembered how he had taken Hays to
Clarksburg in order to board the coach to Washington.
It was on this trip that he had met Henry Clay, the
colorful Senator from Kentucky, who had managed
to squeeze the Missouri Compromise into law.

As Tom remembered the occasion, he wondered
if Hays would recommend him. In a way, he was

almost certain that he would because he knew that
Hays had known, and appreciated, many Jacksons.
Even so, he was deeply concerned.

News of the West Point vacancy spread rapidly, and
so when Tom arrived in Weston to take the qualifying
examination, he met three other candidates. They
were Joe Lightburn, Johnson N. Camden, and
Gibson J. Butcher.

Since Camden was too young, he was immediately
disqualified. As Jackson faced the tests, he was glad
that one of them was in his special field—mathematics.
He felt that he would do well on that test. But as he
studied the questions, his heart sank. Several of them
were too hard for him. He knew nothing about either
algebra or trigonometry. Indeed, he had hardly even
heard of those subjects.

After the tests, Tom went home to await the verdict.
Each hour of waiting was painful. Again and again
he awakened in the early hours of the morning and
paced the floor. He was haunted by the question: did
I solve that problem correctly? In time, the results
came in. Due to his high grade on the mathematics
test, Gibson J. Butcher, one of the three candidates
received a letter of congratulations from John C.
Spencer, the Secretary of War. It was dated April 19,
1842. The letter informed him that he had been given
a conditional appointment to West Point.

Tom wished him well, but he was heartbroken. It
seemed that every door he faced had been securely
bolted against him.

8

Destination: West Point

Although spring was in the air there was no spring in Tom's heart. Due to his own negligence, he had not done well in the examinations that would have opened the doors for him into West Point. True, he was a Jackson. But as he labored for his Uncle at his old job as an overseer, he became utterly convinced that he was not worthy of that name. His one certainty was that he would never amount to anything.

Both his feet felt as heavy as lead.

In addition to his discouragement from having failed the examinations, his old physical troubles returned. Ever since his trip to the Mississippi, he had stomach trouble. This trouble, he believed, could be offset by sitting or standing ramrod straight whenever he ate. Also, he was convinced that one side of his body was larger than the other side. To help equalize them, he developed the habit of holding his arm out straight with his palm opened in a vertical position.

Eighteen forty-two turned out to be an exciting year. A dispute had arisen with England over the slave-ship *Creole* which, while heading for the United States, was hijacked by the slaves and forced to sail to Nassau where the British governor both accepted and announced that the slaves were free.

American newspapers, especially those in the south, screamed that the hijacking was an act of piracy. The war of 1812 with England had been sparked by England's interference with American shipping. *Would the Creole affair explode into a similar war?*

Tom often heard the subject discussed, but he never made a comment. His mind concentrated only on one subject: West Point.

While watching Uncle Robinson set a fence post, the kindly old man studied him curiously. "What's da matter wid you, Massa Tom?" he asked. "Seems dat you tink you's carryin' da whole world on yo' shoulders."

"Uncle Robinson," replied Tom, shaking his head. "I don't feel that way at all."

"Den what's troublin' you?" He peered into Tom's face and smiled.

"I'm disappointed because I wanted to go to West Point."

"Ah see." Robinson wrinkled his brow. "Dat shouldn't bodder you nohow. Your ma told you dat you should 'mount to somethin'. But you can't 'mount to no nothin' unless you does what de good Lord wants you to do. Me and my wife ain't got nothin'. We's jist poor slaves, but we's happy. And why is we happy? Because we does de work of de Lord!"

"What do you do?" Tom was curious.

"We goes to church. We works hard. And we pray."

"For whom do you pray?" Tom cocked his head.

"Oh, we prays for everyone, 'specially for dose dat

are sick, and dose who've been mean to us."

"Do you ever pray for Uncle Cummins?"

"Deed we do."

"Do you think your prayin' does any good?"

Robinson's jaw sagged. "Why yo' asked dat?" he cried. "Deed it does! Me and Aunt Robinson prays for him ebry day."

"Will you pray that I'll get to enroll at West Point?"

Robinson was silent. "Deed we will. But we won't pray dat you go dere. No, suh! We'll pray dat you gets to go dere if'n it's de Lawd's will."

"Thank you. I believe in your prayers." Tom smiled.

"And 'member when we prays togedder, we has power. De Good Book says, 'If two or tree of you shall agree on earth as touchin' any ting dat dey shall ask, it shall be done for dem of my Fodder which is in hebben.' "

Tom laughed.

Back home, Tom looked up that passage in the Bible. He found it in Matthew 18:19. As he studied it he smiled. There was no one in whom he had more confidence than in Uncle or Aunt Robinson. He was confident that they knew God.

Relaxed, Tom began to think about other things. At the table, the conversation turned to politics. President William Henry Harrison who started his term the year before on March 4, 1841, had gone out to buy vegetables for the White House without his overcoat, and had caught cold. Unable to rest because of the endless crowds of office seekers, he developed pneumonia and died on April 4th, one month after his inauguration. His death meant that his Vice-President, John Tyler, also a Virginian, was the new president.

"Do you think President Tyler will be a good president?" asked Tom.

"Who knows?" replied Cummins. "He faces many problems. The National debt already is $26,601,226." He smiled grimly. "Tom, that's a lot of money. He also faces the problem of slavery. Congressman Joshua Giddings just presented an anti-slavery bill to the House. Fortunately, it was defeated by a vote of 125 to 65. But the pressure against slavery is mounting. Yankees like William Lloyd Garrison are using the mails to make trouble, I still have a copy of the first editorial he printed in the *Liberator*. Just sit here while I get it."

Minutes later, Cummins returned with a worn newspaper. After spreading it on the table, he said, "This is not a copy of his paper. But it contains the heart of his first editorial. Just listen:"

> *On this subject I do not wish to think, or speak, or write with moderation. No! no! Tell a man whose house is on fire to give a moderate alarm; tell him to moderately rescue his wife from the hands of a ravisher; tell the mother to gradually extricate her babe from the fire into which it has fallen — but urge me not to use moderation in a cause like the present. I am in earnest — I will not equivocate — I will not excuse — I will not retreat a single inch — AND I WILL BE HEARD.*

"That man's on fire; and the worst part of it is that he's settin' other fanatics on fire. Soon, unless a miracle takes place, our old way of life will be gone. It will be gone with the wind." He strode angrily from the table.

Tom continued to grieve over his misfortune. Over and over again, he wailed, "I'm a failure. I'll never amount to anything. It would have been better if I had never been born. I have a bad stomach, I'm slow to learn—and one side of me is larger than the other side."

He was bemoaning his fate during the first week of June when Butcher showed up. "Has West Point let out?" exclaimed Tom.

"No," replied Butcher with emphasis. "It's still going on. I just quit."

"Quit? Did you get permission to leave?" Tom's jaw sagged, and he stared with unbelief.

"No. I just left. West Point's a horrible place! The cadets have to do everything by routine. You have to get up at a certain time. You have to go to bed at a certain time. You have to make your bed in a certain way. You have to salute all your superiors. And if you do anything wrong, or neglect to follow one of your assignments, you will receive a demerit. I'd rather be dead than be there." He shook his head.

"What are you going to do?"

"I don't know. But there is one thing which I won't do. I won't go back to West Point!"

Within half an hour after Butcher had gone, Tom hurried to his uncle. After explaining what his friend had done, he all but exploded with a question. "Uncle Cummins, do you think I could fill the vacancy he has created?"

Cummins bit his lip and rubbed his bald spot. "You—you might be able to do just that." He spoke with increasing confidence. "But if you're goin' to make the attempt, you'd better hurry. Time is of the essence as Judge Jackson used to say."

"What should I do?"

"First, get Butcher to write a letter to Hays which you can deliver to the Congressman in person. Then get some letters of recommendation. Next, head for Washington, and do so lickety-split."

Butcher complied with Tom's request immediately. He wrote:

It is with deep regret that I have to now send you my

*resignation as a "Cadet" in the West Point Military Academy.
. . . I did not know as much about the institution when I
applied for the appointment as I know now. . . . I have only
to regret the disappointment I have made, especially having
disappointed you. . . . You will please communicate my
resignation to the Secretary of War and if consistent with your
view remain my friend. Mr. Jackson will deliver this letter
to you, who is an applicant for the appointment. . . .*

After Uncle Cummins read the letter, he said,
"That's excellent. But now you need some letters of
recommendation."

All of those Tom called on were generous. One
flattering letter was signed by thirteen friends. The
signatures included Colonel Withers, Tom's former
teacher, Peregrine Hays, son of the Congressman,
Richard Riddell, M.D., and others.

With these and other letters, Tom prepared to go.
As he gathered his homespun clothes, Aunt Robinson
said, "Now Massa Tom, you'd better let me iron
them things. It'll be bad 'nough for you to show up
in homespun, but if they ain't ironed, it'll be worse."

Tom's next obstacle was to get to Washington on
time. Cummins suggested that he ride a horse to
Clarksburg along with a slave on another horse,
"Then, after you've caught the stage, Sam can lead
your horse home." Dressed in his finest homespun,
and carrying two saddlebags loaded with his things,
Tom set out for Clarksburg.

As he galloped along, he could feel his heart beating.
*Was this the beginning of a glorious career? Would he be
remembered in the same way in which Francis Marion was
remembered?* Several cities and a county in western
Virginia had honored Marion by using his name.
Undoubtedly he would never do that well, but he felt
deeply that he would at last amount to something.

After he dismounted at the stage depot, he was

alarmed to learn that the stage had already left. "When does the next one leave?" he demanded.

"In three days."

"Three days!" gasped Tom. "I can't wait for three days!"

The manager glanced at the clock. "If you hurry, you could catch up with it at Grafton," he suggested.

Frantically Tom and Sam headed down the road. "Massa Tom, we'll catch him. I knows a few short-cuts," assured Sam.

Since the horses were already tired, Tom hated to rush them. Still. . . . Finally, at Grafton, about eighteen miles east of Clarksburg, they overtook the stage. Then at the Green Valley Depot, just east of Cumberland, Maryland, he changed from the stage to a train. This was the first train he had ever seen, and as he watched the engine wallowing in its own steam, he was stirred with amazement.

Presently the whistle screeched. He was on his way to Washington! Sitting by a window he watched the country slip by. After the conductor punched his ticket, he pinched himself to make certain he wasn't dreaming. Everything was so unreal.

On June 17th he stepped out of the train into the nation's capital. With its immense population of 15,000, it was the largest city he had even dared to imagine. He was utterly overwhelmed, even though most of the streets were full of mud along with dozens of pigs that meandered about, and cooled off in the numerous ruts and puddles.

Tom didn't have time for the sights. Without hesitating he stopped a cab and directed it to the home of C ngressman Hays. As he stepped in he noticed that the driver's eyes focused a little too sharply on his homespun and country haircut; but with effort, he merely swallowed, and said nothing. *He might be*

a country bumpkin, but he was on his way to West Point!
Moreover he was a Jackson.

Congressman Hays was delighted to see him.

"I want to fill Gibson Butcher's place at West Point," explained Tom. "I've brought some documents."

"I know all about it," replied Hays, smiling. "I just got two letters recommending you. One is loaded with thirty-one signatures." He smiled. "Your neighbors think a lot of you!"

"Do—do you think I c-could be a-accepted?"

"That's not really up to me. However, I will recommend you. After lunch we'll go over to the Capitol and see the Secretary of War, John C. Spencer."

Following a simple lunch, Tom, along with Congressman Hays went to the War office. Spencer studied him carefully, and wanting to give help for the hard times ahead, humorously commented, "Sir, you have a good name. And the first man who insults you, knock him down, and have it charged to my account."

Congressman Hays pled with Tom to remain with him in the city for a few days. This, Tom was reluctant to do, for he knew that he should start cramming for the inevitable examinations ahead. But he agreed to linger for a day so that he might climb the unfinished Capitol dome and view the sights.

Standing with Tom, his host pointed across the Potomac to the magnificent home of Captain Robert E. Lee. "He's a talented man," he commented. To the west, Tom viewed the hazy outline of the Blue Ridge Mountains stretching across his beloved Virginia. In the southwest he noted the plains of Manassas.

9

Breaking The Underdog Cycle

As Tom entered the school of his dreams, he officially registered under the name Thomas Jonathan Jackson. This proved to be a wise move, since there was another Jackson cadet named Thomas K.

On his first day—June 20, 1842—at the United States Military Academy, located on the west bank of the Hudson, just south of Storm King Mountain, and nearly fifty miles north of New York City, Tom was nervous. Four young plebes were conversing with one another when they noticed him being escorted to his quarters by a cadet sergeant.

Dabney Maury, one of the group, already a college graduate at twenty, remembered the occasion well. "The personal appearance of the stranger was so remarkable as to attract the attention of several of us, who were standing near and chatting together."

Tom's grey homespun, heavy brogans, wagoner's hat, and worn saddle bags carried across his shoulder, were indeed unusual—especially to a group that came from at least middle-class families. But Maury also noticed his sturdy step and what he called his cold bright gray eyes, (although his eyes were actually blue). "That fellow looks as if he has come to stay."

Studying himself in a mirror, Tom saw a clean-shaven face, stubborn chin, high cheek bones, studious eyes, sloping forehead. Unlike his father who was remembered as moderately short, Tom was five feet, ten and a half inches tall. But as he viewed himself, he wondered if he would ever make it through the courses. The competition, he feared, was beyond him. George McClellan, for example, was from a wealthy Philadelphia family. He was an excellent sudent, having graduated from college at age 15. He had even gone to Europe to observe the Crimean War and was allowed to enter West Point two years before the required age.

In contrast, Tom had never even seen a college, had only been in school a few months—and was a near-penniless orphan. Lifting his eyes to the door of his barrack room, he read a notice that intimidated him.

Bedstead, against door — Trunks, under iron bedsteads — Lamps, clean on mantel — Dress caps, neatly arranged behind doors — Books, neatly arranged on shelf farthest from door — Broom hanging behind door — Drawing books, under shelf farthest from door — Muskets in gun rack and locks sprung — Bayonets, in scabbards — Accouterments, hanging over muskets — Sabers, cutlasses, swords, hanging over the muskets — Candle box for scrubbing utensils, against wall under shelf nearest door and fireplace — Clothes, neatly hung on pegs over bedsteads — Mattress and blankets, neatly folded — Orderly board, over mantle — Chairs when not used, under tables — Orderlies of rooms are held responsible for the observance of the above mentioned arrangements.

Tom was used to having a slave do such things as make his bed and tidy his room. Unbelieving, he reread the notice, and shook his head. Now he thought he understood why Butcher had left!

The class schedule was even more dismaying. From September until June, he was to have three-hour daily classes in math. After a quick gulp, he noted that he would have to study English four hours every day over the same period. French—and why should he study French?—required four hours every other day, from January to June. The one easy class was the one in which instructions were given in the use of small arms. That class, unfortunately, was only for an hour a day, and lasted a mere 23 weeks.

Considering what he faced, Tom felt like a man who was being led into a medieval torture chamber. The printed description of the English course alone was enough to curl the hairs on the back of his neck. It stated: "English Grammar, including Etymological and Rhetorical Exercises, Composition, Declamation, and Geography of the United States."

Tom was shuddering over this when a bugle sounded.

"What's that?" he asked a cadet who had just stepped into the barracks.

"Supper," he replied. "Make sure your hair is combed, your nails are clean, your shoes are shined, and your collar and tie are adjusted just right. Then follow me. We have to get in line and march to the mess hall."

"Where will we sit?"

"With the plebes."

"And who are they?" Tom's jaw sagged.

"The word *plebe* is Latin. In the days of the Caesars, it referred to the lower classes," replied the cadet.

"Are we from a low class of people?" asked Tom with a chuckle.

"No, all freshmen are plebes."

"And what happens if my bed isn't properly made, or if I don't hang my clothes on the right peg?"

"Then you'll get a demerit, and if you get too many demerits you'll be expelled from the school. But now we'd better get in line and be ready to march."

Along with the others, Tom marched into the mess hall, took his seat at the proper time, sat ramrod straight, ate his food, marched out with the group, and then returned to his barracks. His first week at West Point was one of acute agony. Not only were all of his subjects, with the exception of that of handling small arms, beyond him; but, in addition, there were countless drills and inspections. Occasionally he was tempted to follow Butcher's example and resign. There were, however, three things which sustained him.

One of these was a line in the notebook he had filled with maxims. The maxim that gave him the most courage was the one he had written in capital letters:

YOU MAY BE WHATEVER YOU RESOLVE TO BE

Another courage sustainer was his memory of his mother's last words on her deathbed. He could still see the look in her faded eyes when she said, "I'm expecting each of you to amount to something. Someday you will also be called Home. When that time comes may it be said that the world is better because you lived."

The third thing that sustained him was prayer. Each evening he continued to repeat the prayer based on Psalm 4:8 which begins: "Now I lay me down to sleep . . ."

At the end of his first year, out of a class of 72, his grades nearly scraped the bottom—especially in French. His record showed his standing was as follows:

Order of merit in French—70
Order of merit in mathematics—45
Order of general merit—51
Demerits—15.

Tom was thankful that out of 223 cadets in the entire school, his order of conduct was 38. The major thing he was learning was discipline, and strict obedience to orders from his superiors. Although he was getting by, he wasn't satisfied with his grades, so he developed the habit of studying by the fireplace at night in the winter months, and by an open window during the long summer days. As a result, his grades improved.

He increased his standing in mathematics from number 45 in a class of 72, to number 18 in a class of 78. He made similar advances in other subjects. His position in English zoomed to number 55. But his demerits increased to 26.

All of Tom's demerits were not deserved. Some cadets played tricks on others in order to increase their demerits. One of these focused his mischief on Tom. Upon examining his musket, which he kept spotlessly clean, Tom discovered that it had been replaced by a dirty one. Annoyed, he approached his captain.

"This is not my musket," he said, pointing to the dirty one. "I have a secret mark on mine to identify it. Someone has exchanged them so that I'll get a few more demerits." He frowned.

Eventually the culprit was discovered by the fact that he was shouldering Tom's musket with the secret mark. Thoroughly annoyed, Tom decided the cadet should be court marshalled.

"Have mercy on him," pled the captain.

"No," persisted Tom. "If a cadet is willing to play such a trick he isn't worthy of being graduated from West Point."

Others pled that he drop the case; and, eventually he did. But time proved that Tom was right. The thief was later convicted of "disgraceful conduct," and was expelled shortly before he was due to graduate. After a while he got into serious trouble with the law.

Tom continued to jot maxims in his notebook. One emphasized a trait that made him prefer to be a loner. It stated: "It is not desirable to have a large number of intimate friends; you may have many acquaintances, but few intimate friends." Those who knew him best, agreed that he followed this maxim. His favorite recreation was to go for long solitary walks and to meditate alone.

He wrote to Laura regularly. Besides being his sister, she remained one of his best friends, and he often related his most intimate thoughts to her. In a letter to her dated January 28, 1844, he was extremely frank. "I am almost homesick and expect to continue so until I can have a view of my native mountains. . . .

"If no change takes place in the army, and I continue to progress in my class as well as I have so far, my pay when I leave this institution will be about one thousand dollars a year; though fate may decree that I shall graduate in the lower part of my class, in which case I shall have to go into the infantry and would receive only seven hundred and fifty dollars a year. But I feel very confident that unless fortune frowns . . . more than it has yet, I shall graduate in the upper half of my class and high enough in it to enter the Dragoons. But be that as it may, I intend to remain in the army no longer than I can get rid of it with honor, and means, to commence some professional business at home."

During the summer of 1844, Tom was given permission to go home on furlough. While visiting

with his cousin Sylvanus White, he remarked to him:
"I tell you I had to work hard. Not for all Lewis
County would I fail to go back to West Point. I am
going to make a man out of myself if I live. I can do
anything I will to do."

Tom arranged to spend half the summer with Laura
at the place where she was living with relatives in
Randolph County. As the weeks passed, the lessons
he had learned at West Point came into perspective
like sections of a puzzle. In addition, he learned that
he was being molded by things he had learned *outside*
of class, and by the general atmosphere of the school.
Indeed, he discovered that some of the things he
learned outside of class were more valuable than what
he learned in class. This came into sharp focus on a
certain Sunday morning.

Having agreed to accompany Miss Caroline Harris
to church, he made certain that his boots glistened,
that the creases in his trousers were razor-sharp, and
that his cadet uniform was utterly spotless. While he
was riding by her side, his horse slipped on a stone
as they crossed the West Fork at Withers' Ford.
Pitched into the three-foot stream, he was utterly
soaked. But without saying a word, he caught the
horse, remounted—and continued on.

Leading Caroline through the front door of the
Broad Run Baptist Church, Tom ignored his dripping
clothes and sat by her side during the entire service.

Commenting on this event later, Tom's cousin,
Sylvanus White, remarked, "Tom was the most polite
and precise man I ever saw."

The atmosphere at West Point was slowly shaping
Tom's spirit into the formidable characteristic of a
solid stone wall.

Tom returned from his furlough and was appointed
a cadet sergeant on June 25, 1844. Yes, he was on

his way. His plebe days were over! However, he continued to feel that he was an underdog, He realized that most of the cadets were able to learn much faster than he. Also, his long solitary walks continued to make him an object of scorn.

Even though it was hard to learn, he gnawed at his books until he mastered them. Then he crunched their bones and lapped their blood until they became a part of his being.

At the end of his third year, his grades had dramatically improved. He triumphantly studied his card. It indicated that he had reached a higher rung on his self-determined ladder. His place was now in the upper one-third of the 62 class members! His card read:

> Order of general merit—20
> Order of merit in philosophy—11
> Order of merit in chemistry—25
> Order of merit in drawing—59
> Order on conduct roll—1 in 204
> Demerits—0.

While Tom burned his candles late during his fourth year, he often thought of what he would do when he received his degree. The newspapers supplied broad hints. Headlines indicated that war was brewing between the United States and Mexico.

Tom had no longing to go to war; but he had learned to be obedient—and was ready.

10

Road To Mexico

Tom faced his fourth and final year at West Point with the determination to make even higher grades than he had achieved the previous year. Since it was still harder for him to learn than it was for many others, he consistently sat up late with his books.

During that year Tom took courses in logic and moral law. He became especially fond of Hedges' *Elements of Logic*, and Wayland's *Elements of Moral Science*. He believed the study of morality to be especially important. Confiding in Laura, he wrote that he considered this science preferable to any other in the West Point course.

By the end of the year, Tom was 5th among the 60 taking this course.

Tom's mind frequently turned to the country of Mexico. He remembered how Sam Houston, then president of the Republic of Texas, had told him a great deal about the situation with Mexico, and had detailed the battle of the Alamo. Then, too, he had never forgotten how the determined Houston had advised him to go to college. President Houston's encouragement had been a big factor in Tom's going to West Point. From that time on, Tom had watched every bit of news which came out of Texas.

Houston remained president until 1844. During his term of office, and later, he continued to insist that Texas be admitted to the Union. His idea incensed the Mexican Government. Its authorities declared that if Texas entered the Union, Mexico would declare war on the United States.

Facing the possibility that he could be ordered to Mexico in the event of war, Tom gritted his teeth to keep his mind from the headlines. Late one evening, unable to fall asleep, he began to systematically analyze himself. Although he was good at mathematics and artillery, for some unknown reason he was not up to his classmates in mechanical ability. When marching, he frequently stepped on the heels of those in front of him. His best talent, he decided, was to understand the abstract. Knowing this, a fellow cadet teased that he would be a chess player. That statement haunted him. It was a discouraging thought, for in time of war, of what value would a chess player be?

In the fall of 1845, President Polk sent John Slidell to Mexico with instructions to offer Mexico $25,000,000 if they would sell New Mexico and California to the United States and accept the Rio Grande as the boundary between Mexico and Texas.

When Slidell reached the capital, he found that Mexico was in the midst of revolution. Because of this, neither the old nor the new president would see him. They feared making negotiations with the United States.

Dismayed, Slidell recommended that Mexico

should be "chastised." President Polk had already stationed General Zachary Taylor with 3000 men on the Nueces River. He then ordered him to advance to the Rio Grande, approximately one hundred miles to the south. Mexico retaliated. This caused Congress to declare war on Mexico on May 13, 1846.

As headlines widened, Tom was certain he would be sent to either Mexico or Texas, but by sheer determination, he kept his mind on his studies.

Finally, Tom took his last West Point examination. Then he waited anxiously to see where he stood. When results were posted, Tom learned that in a graduating class of 59, he numbered 17th from the top.

On July 1st, Tom, along with all his classmates, was given the brevet rank of second lieutenant. "Brevet" meant that they would have the rank of lieutenant but not the pay, and they would have limited exercise of rank.

Tom's first assignment was to report to Francis Taylor at Fort Columbus on Governor's Island, New York. As he studied the order, he realized at once that he was headed for Mexico. Though no one knew his opinion of the controversial war, his training at West Point had prepared him for absolute, complete and unswerving obedience.

Accompanying Captain Taylor, along with his thirty men and forty horses, the new "Second Lieutenant" Jackson boarded ship at Pittsburgh, sailed down the Ohio, and then the Mississippi to New Orleans. From New Orleans, he took his first sea voyage to Point Isabel at the place where the Rio Grande empties into the sea on the east coast of Mexico. There, Jackson had nothing to do but to listen to the stories of others who had been in the battles of Monterrey and Palo Alto.

"We had to take Monterrey block by block,"

exulted one who had been there. Jackson burst out: "Oh, how I envy you men who've been in battle! If I could only be in one, just one."

But instead of seeing action, T. J. Jackson remained stuck at Isabel. Often alone with his thoughts, his mind frequently skipped back to Parson Weems' *Life of Francis Marion* which he had all but devoured in his youth.

Born into a courageous family in South Carolina, Marion was said to be "not larger than a New England lobster, and might easily have been put in a quart pot." In addition, both his knees and ankles were malformed. Yet Marion later proved that men could live on very little and that there was often a way out of most difficult circumstances.

Jackson was walking slowly toward his tent, daydreaming about the events in Marion's life, according to Weems' account, when he noticed Captain Taylor and D. H. Hill strolling along engaged in earnest conversation. "There's Lieutenant Jackson," he overheard Taylor say. "If the course at West Point had been a year longer, he would have been graduated at the head of his class."

The comment sent chills down Jackson's spine. But the observation also made him ask himself, *how can I achieve advancement while stationed at this place?* Then suddenly Captain Taylor approached him: "Prepare to leave tomorrow," snapped the officer after a vigorous salute.

"Yes, Sir!" replied Jackson, as he returned the salute.

"General Winfield Scott has received orders to take Vera Cruz and then head for Mexico City." Taylor's words were crisp.

"Yes, Sir!" repeated Jackson with increased enthusiasm.

Forcing himself to remain calm—at least to appear that way—Jackson returned to his tent. His heart was pounding. *He, Thomas Jonathan Jackson, was about to see action—and he was about to see it on the way to Mexico City, the city of the great Montezuma. Better yet, he would be under the command of Old Fuss and Feathers Scott himself.*

That night Tom had to remind himself to kneel at his bed and pray.

11

A New Beginning

Tom Jackson had heard incredible stories about Winfield Scott ever since he started at West Point. "Not only does 'Old Fuss and Feathers' stand six-feet-four in his stocking feet, but he also has immense shoulders and sledgehammer fists," reported one of his admirers.

"True, the old boy's conceited. Crows like a rooster, But he has a right to do so! He's never lost a battle. Was the hero in the Battle of Lundy's Lane in the War of 1812. Sure, he loves parades and wears all the gold braid he's entitled to. (That's the reason they call him Old Fuss and Feathers.) But in spite of his swagger, and lips that sag at the corners, he delivers the goods. Yes, he always—always—delivers the goods. I'd be honored to fight under his command."

Jackson was impressed. But he knew Vera Cruz was a walled city, protected from the sea by San Juan d'Ulloa, a fortress that had withstood the guns of the French fleet. Its high coral walls, faced with granite,

seemed as formidable as Gibraltar. In addition, it was
a cesspool of yellow fever. He wondered how Old Fuss
and Feathers would take Vera Cruz.

While Jackson wondered what Scott would do, the
completely confident Lieutenant General assembled
his staff. It included Major Jubal Early, Captain
Robert E. Lee, Captain Joseph E. Johnson—and
George B. McClellan, the number two graduate in
Jackson's class at West Point.

Along with 10,000 others, Jackson awaited action.
Instead of attacking Vera Cruz from the front, Scott
and his men sailed beyond the city with its fort, and
waded ashore several miles to the south. The men
faced little opposition.

Scott brought in huge guns, some of them weighing
over three tons. Soon there were artillery duels, and
Jackson at last tasted war. He carried out his part of
the siege obediently and bravely, and higher officers
took notice of him. Once a cannonball missed him
by only five paces. Under the siege, Vera Cruz soon
surrendered. Jackson later was cited for "gallant and
meritorious conduct at the siege of Vera Cruz" and
was promoted to brevet first lieutenant.

With Vera Cruz taken, the door was now opened
to head for Mexico City, 200 miles away. Scott divided
his forces into two groups, one headed by General
William Worth, and the other by General David
Twiggs. Jackson was assigned to Twiggs' command
which preceded Worth's regiments. The first city to
subdue on their way was Jalapa, seventy-five miles
to the west.

Jalapa offered no resistance and Jackson was so
fascinated with this four-thousand-foot-high city he
began to learn Spanish while there. Then came more
action. The Americans continued west with increasing
rapidity. Though outnumbered, they were better

equipped and better trained, and were easy victors at Contreras and Churubusco. But after a two-week armistice, they bogged down just outside Mexico City.

The problem was the hilltop "castle" at Chapultepec. It had the advantage of crowning the summit of a hill. The solid buildings were the center of acute interest to both sides. In that they had been used for a military college since 1833, the Mexicans held them in almost sacred reverence. And since the Americans considered them to be either a castle or a fortress and viewed them as *the* gateway to Mexico City, they were determined to subdue the place. On September 11 Captain Robert E. Lee had cannon arranged to bombard Chapultepec's southern walls. The next day, they began an intense bombardment that lasted fourteen hours.

Jackson led his men onto the left of the attacking line. But they were in a tight situation. He was on a road swept with grape and canister (cast-iron cannon balls). Thousands of muskets from the Castle above kept pouring bullets down like hail. Almost at once one of his cannon was knocked out, and many of his horses were killed. Terrified, his men cowered behind any protection they could find.

Taking in the situation at a glance, Jackson paced back and forth while he shouted, "There's no danger. See! I'm not hit." But his bravado did not convince the men. With bullets and grape swishing all around and their ears filled with the boom of enemy cannon, they refused to expose themselves.

Motioning to the one sergeant who was defying the danger, Jackson moved a cannon across a ditch. Horrified by what he was seeing, General Worth, fearing the cannon would be lost, sent him an order to retreat to their line of infantry.

Jackson sent back a reply: "With one company of

regulars as a support, I could carry the work.'' Worth then moved a whole brigade forward.

In the midst of the fight, Captain John B. Magruder rode up. Almost instantly his horse was killed. But he recovered quickly and helped Jackson get another gun into position. Soon, a pair of cannon were being swabbed, loaded, fired; swabbed, loaded, fired. Within minutes the Mexican guns in that area were silenced.

Eventually, Chapultepec was taken and Mexico City surrendered.

As a reward for his skill and bravery, Jackson was made a brevet major. His progress in rank had been rapid. He had arrived in Mexico as a brevet second lieutenant. Next he was made a permanent second lieutenant. Following this, on August 20, he became a first lieutenant; and on the same day he was promoted to the rank of brevet captain. Then, on September 13, 1847, he was made a brevet major.

The young man from Clarksburg had risen like mercury in a thermometer on a hot day. Studying himself in a mirror he was quite satisfied. Yes, he was a Jackson!

Even though a peace treaty had not yet been signed, the War with Mexico was over. Jackson, along with other officers, was quartered in the National Palace. There, he lived in luxury. Each day he slept until nine, had a cup of chocolate brought to his bed by a peasant girl, and then spent the rest of his time drilling and viewing the sights.

The peace treaty was finally signed on February 2, 1848. Many Americans wanted the United States to annex all of Mexico. But President Polk insisted that Mexico should merely give up the territory the United States had originally requested. That included the area north of the Rio Grande—New Mexico and

California. This land, surrendered by Mexico, amounted to 525,000 square miles. It eventually became the states of California, Nevada, Utah, New Mexico, Arizona, and parts of both Colorado and Wyoming. The United States Government paid Mexico $15,000,000 for this land.

The war was not popular with everyone. One who disagreed was Abraham Lincoln, who first took his seat in Congress after the war with Mexico had just concluded. The conflict had cost the United States $27,000,000 together with the lives of nearly 13,000 soldiers. Convinced that it had been an unjust war, Lincoln got to his feet, and pointing at President Polk, called him "a bewildered, confounded, and miserably perplexed man."

Agreeing with the former rail-splitter, Senator Corwin of Ohio, was brusk: "Were I a Mexican, I would say to the invader: 'We welcome you with bloody hands to hospitable graves.' "

Although both Lincoln and Corwin failed to be reelected because of their stand, most Americans rejoiced at the United States' victory and especially the more than half a million square miles that had been added to its possessions.

In contrast to Abraham Lincoln, Democrat Stephen A Douglas, quoted Frederick the Great: "Take possession first and negotiate afterward." He underlined that idea by thundering: "That is precisely what President Polk has done. He has taken possession and proposed to negotiate."

A far more belligerent stand was taken by Jefferson Davis, the fill-in senator from Mississippi. This slender six-footer had been wounded in the foot, but had remained in the saddle until victory was achieved. Rising to address the Senate, Davis was quite pointed: "I hold that in a just war we conquered the larger

portion of Mexico and that to it we have a title which
has been regarded as valid ever since man existed in
a social condition—the title of conquest. It seems to
me that the question now is, how much shall we keep,
how much shall we give up, and that Mexico cedes
nothing."

He further suggested that the United States should
take Yucatan, and that if England tried to annex it,
the United States should even declare war if necessary
in order to keep it.

Senator Davis' stand was popular. On the last day
of 1850 he was reelected to the Senate for a full six-
year term.

Major Jackson had strong opinions about the
"justness" of the war. But he made it a point that
none of them should appear in print. He was a soldier;
and he always kept in mind that he had made an oath
to remain obedient regardless of his private thoughts.

While still living in Mexico City, he continued to
study Spanish; and through experience he learned that
the best way to acquire vocabulary was to read books
printed in Spanish. With the help of a dictionary at
his elbow, he read Lord Chesterfield's letters in
Spanish, several of Shakespeare's plays, and
Humboldt's *History of Mexico*. Soon, he was fluent in
the language.

Thinking that he could be stationed in Mexico for
the rest of his life, Tom teased Laura that he might
make his life a little more enjoyable by marrying "a
Spanish maiden." That idea, however, was only a
temporary fancy.

He kept busy doing other things. He explained his
daily life to Laura: ". . . when not on duty I generally
pay a visit after supper or tea. Among the families
I visit are some of the first in the republic. . . . Owing

to my knowledge of the language . . . I pass my time more agreeably than the greater portion of the officers in the army . . .''

But Jackson's mind was not completely concentrated on Spanish, Mexican girls, or the sights. Night after night he was haunted by thoughts about Christianity. This trend of thinking was encouraged by Colonel Frank Taylor, the commander of his artillery regiment. Sometimes in the early hours of the morning, he remembered the Christian witness of the Robinsons—his Uncle Cummins' slaves. Although owned by a white man, they always managed a smile. And frequently his mind went back to his mother's deathbed. He still remembered her final words: ''The secret of living right is to stay close to the Lord. You must learn to pray. Pray when you go to bed. Pray when you get up. Pray during the day. And have faith. You must believe in the One who made you . . .''

Thinking of his past life, Jackson remembered only one definite sin that he had committed. And that sin was the lie he told his men when he assured them that there was no danger of being hit at Chapultepec even though bullets were whizzing all abound him. But he was comforted by the fact that he had observed the Sabbath, and had attended worship services whenever possible. And yet there was one matter that festered in his heart. That matter was spelled out in Romans 10:10.

Opening his Bible, he reread the passage: *"For with the heart man believeth unto righteousness; and with the mouth confession is made unto salvation."* Those final words condemned him, for he realized that he had never openly said to anyone: "I'm a Christian." Indeed, he hadn't even been baptized.

While struggling with his spiritual need, Jackson's career reached an abrupt turn. The peace treaty with Mexico was signed. The American flag was pulled down and replaced by the Mexican flag, and he was returned to the United States and assigned to Fort Hamilton, on Long Island, about ten miles from New York City.

There he kept busy preparing a comfortable place to live. But even while he was installing furniture, he was conscious that the Holy Spirit was urging him to take a public stand for Christ and become an out-and-out Christian.

Providentially, he wandered into a used bookstore and found a copy of Weems' *Life of Francis Marion.* Returning to his room with his favorite book, he turned to the last chapter, and read about his hero's death.

"Some," said Marion, "have spoken of death as a *leap in the dark*; but for my part, I look on it as a welcome *resting place*, where virtuous old age may throw down his pains and aches, wipe off his old scores, and begin anew on an innocent and happy state that shall last forever.''

When Marion was near his end, seeing his lady weeping by his bedside, he gave her a look of great tenderness, and said, ''My dear, weep not for me, I am not afraid to die; for, thank God, I can lay my hand on my heart and say, that since I came to man's estate, I have never intentionally done wrong to any.''

Deeply moved, Jackson decided that he would take a public stand for Christ by being baptized. But where would this be done, and which denomination would he join? He finally decided to be baptized in the little St. John's Episcopal Church across the street from the fort. The ceremony was performed on Sunday, April 29, 1849, with a prior understanding that he would not become an Episcopalian, although he admired the Episcopalians.

Robert E. Lee was an Episcopalian, but Jackson favored the Presbyterians, Methodists and Baptists. Pastors of those denominations had influenced him during his youth.

This public stand for Christ was a new beginning for Thomas Jonathan Jackson.

12

A New Purpose

Now that he had declared himself a Christian, Major Jackson was happier than he had ever been. His new commitment meant that his sins had been forgiven, that he could experience Divine guidance, that he was on his way to heaven—and that his main task on earth was to introduce others to Jesus Christ. *Ah but where would he start?* That question was easy to answer. He would start with his own sister, Laura!

Thinking about her, he remembered how devout she had been years before. She had often urged him to accept Christ. But as the years passed she had become cold, careless, indifferent. Being diplomatic, and knowing that Laura's daughter Anna Grace was seriously ill, he used that fact as an opener, as he wrote from his heart:

> *I hope that my dear little niece has recovered her health, but do you not think, my dear sister, that her illness, has been the result of a Divine decree? You remember that once you were a professed follower of Christ, and that subsequently you disavowed his cause. This my Dear Sister, I do not believe*

*will go unpunished, unless you return to him. Will you
not do it? You professed religion when quite young, and
possibly could not at that tender age appreciate its bless-
ings. . . . Oh! Sister, do drop your 'Infidel Books'. Come
lead a happy life, and die a happy death. And indeed
I hope to see that day when you will pour forth your
soul in pure prayer. My daily prayers are for your salvation, and some of my prayerful petitions have been
answered, and I hope ere long this will be included.*

In the middle of his twenty-fifth year, Jackson, as
well as his sister Laura, began to have trouble with
his eyes. The Major, fearing that if he started to wear
spectacles he would have to continue wearing them
the rest of his life, developed a special diet for himself
which he explained to Laura. "I have so strictly
adhered to my wholesome diet of stale bread and
plainly dressed meat (having nothing on it but salt)
that I prefer it now to almost anything else."

Sad news came to him in 1849. His uncle Cummins
had been attracted to the California gold rush and had
moved there. But shortly after his arrival, he had
passed away.

Brokenhearted, Tom wrote to Laura: "This is news
that goes to my heart. Uncle was a father to me."

Though still proud that his name was Jackson, Tom
thought less these days about self-glory, He dreamed
less often about having cities named after him, as
Francis Marion had. Now that he was a Christian,
his goal was to be like Jesus Christ.

Compared with his Mexico experiences, life at Fort
Hamilton was humdrum. Tom was given court-
martial duty, and transferred to Indiana, and then
to the primitive outpost of Fort Meade in Florida.

Jackson's spirits drooped as he swatted mosquitoes
and endured the humidity. He longed to be transferred. With effort he kept his mind busy studying

the Bible, and trying to influence Laura. His letters
to her indicate the intensity of this faith.

How *glorious* will it be in that august and heaven-
ordained day to meet with mother, brother, sister,
and father around the shining throne of
Omnipotence; there I wish and hope to meet you,
with a joy that shall never be alloyed with separation.

I believed that God would restore me to perfect
health, and such continues to be my belief . . . yes,
my dear sister, rather than wilfully violate the known
will of God I would forfeit my life; it may seem
strange to you, yet nevertheless such a resolution I
have taken, and I will by it abide.

Returning from a scouting expedition one day,
Jackson found a letter formally addressed to Bvt.
Major Thos. J. Jackson. It was dated February 4,
1851. He hurriedly sat down and ripped it open.

The letter was from F. H. Smith asking if he would be interested in teaching natural and experimental Philosophy at the Virginia Military Institute. The salary he would receive, if elected, would be $1200 a year plus "quarters."

Thoroughly excited about the prospects of teaching, Jackson replied on the 25th, the very day he found the letter awaiting him. His memory lingering on the Blue Ridge Mountains, the magnificent Shenandoah Valley, the rivers crammed with fish, and the days of his childhood, he hastily replied: "I cannot decline so flattering an offer. Please present my name to the Board."

After mailing his reply, he began to pace the floor and pray that God's will be done. This anxiety was increased when he learned that among other candidates being considered were such stalwarts as George McClellan, William S. Rosecrans, Alexander P. Stewart, Gustavus W. Smith, and T. S. Laidley.

There was no need for Jackson to worry. The Board met on March 27, and it was unanimously voted that he be given the position. His Mexican war record, and the fact that he was a Virginian persuaded the Board that he was their man.

Twenty-seven-year-old Jackson moved to Lexington in July.

Eager to learn about the institute, he visited an officer. This man informed Jackson that the Virginia Military Institute was already twelve years old, that it had an eight-acre campus, and made use of a former arsenal which had been built to store the 30,000 muskets that remained from the War of 1812.

Jackson was pleased to learn that the institute was modeled after West Point. Remembering the smart clothes in which the professors dressed at his alma mater, he decided to dress in a similar way. The cadets were impressed by his appearance when he first stepped onto the parade ground.

Although it was a scorching day, he wore an immaculate double-breasted blue coat, white pantaloons, gleaming artillery boots, military cap complete with visor—and white gloves. Ignoring the sweat that saturated his long sideburns draped to his chin, he stood ramrod-straight amidst a knot of spectators on the sidelines as the cadets marched back and forth in response to the barked commands of Cadet Adjutant Thomas T. Munford. As he watched, his mind zoomed back to West Point. He was reliving his own experiences when, during a pause in the drill, a sharp voice from a cadet shouted at him, "Come out of them boots, they are not allowed in this camp."

Startled, Munford glanced at the spectators. When he saw Major Jackson, his heart speeded. Hurrying over to him, he saluted and then apologized.

"That's perfectly all right," replied Jackson. "Continue with the drill. I'm new. In time, I'll learn."

After the drilling, Adjutant Munford handed Jackson a book of cadet regulations. Not wanting to be caught in another awkward position, Jackson all but memorized the regulations.

Jackson soon became accustomed to Lexington, a city which he loved. That fall, in a letter to Laura, he said: "I admire the citizens·very much," and later at the end of the first semester, commented: "I consider [our institute] the most tasty in the state, and I am enjoying myself more that I have done in years."

But happy as he was, his West Point military training trailed him like a shadow, making a unique impression upon people. At a social gathering at Washington College, a student noticed the new teacher and remembered:

"Jackson sat perfectly erect, his back not touching the back of the chair. His large hands were spread out, one on each knee, while the large feet, sticking out at an exact right angle to the leg (the angle seeming to have been determined with mathematical precision), occupied an unwarranted space. Jackson reminded me of a figure recalled by my boyish mind that I had once seen—a rude Egyptian-carved figure of one of the Pharaohs."

A citizen of Lexington was so intrigued by the Major, he commented that he was as "exact as the multiplication table and as full of things military as an arsenal."

During the winter when all the roofs and streets were white with snow, the Superintendent summoned Jackson to his office. Then, after pointing him to a chair, disappeared to attend to an errand. Forgetting that Jackson had arrived precisely on time, and was awaiting his return, he fell into conversation with one of the teachers. Later, when he did remember, he surmised that Jackson had given up and retired to his room. Completely relaxed, he ate his supper and went to bed.

But the next morning, when he stepped into his office, he was shocked to discover that Jackson was still ramrod straight in the same chair he had pointed him to the day before.

"Sir," explained Jackson, "you told me to be seated yesterday and I'm following your orders."

The Superintendent stared. Then he laughed. *Jackson had what it takes to be a great soldier!*

From the day he first arrived in Lexington, Jackson learned that the Protestants were divided into four groups: Presbyterian, Baptist, Episcopal, and Methodist. Determined to align himself with the group that came the closest to his doctrinal beliefs, he visited all four of them.

The venerable Dr. William S. White, pastor of the Presbyterian Church, captured his heart. But since he didn't agree with all the doctrines the Presbyterians taught, he called on Dr. White for an interview. After their conversation, the pastor said, "Well, Major, although your doctrinal theory is not in perfect accord with ours, yet in your practical life you are so good a Presbyterian that I think you should remain with us."

Jackson was received into the Presbyterian Church by profession of faith on November 22, 1851. He

wanted to grow spiritually. He and a friend discussed the way the Israelites in Old Testament times supported the work of the Lord by tithing. Fascinated,

Jackson studied the topic from all **angles. Convinced** that he should become a tither, he **began to give one** tenth of his income to the work of the Lord. Later, he increased this percentage.

A few years later, Jackson was unanimously elected a deacon. In this capacity he seriously accepted his task "to serve tables."

When he was asked to collect gifts for the American Bible Society, he picked up the sheet containing the names of those on whom he should call, and got busy. On his return, he handed the document to the pastor. It included a notation about the sum each had given. Noticing a series of new names penciled in, Dr. White asked, "And what are these?"

"Those at the top," replied Jackson, "are the regulars, and those below are my militia."

A quick examination of the names, indicated that Jackson's "militia" was "free blacks" (those in the community who had purchased their freedom, or who had otherwise been freed). Each had given an offering. Seeing a need, Jackson organized a Sunday school made up of slaves. The group met in the Presbyterian church on Sunday afternoons at 3 o'clock. There were twelve teachers and the attendance averaged nearly eighty.

Always punctual, Jackson closed the doors at exactly three. At first, many were shut out. Those who were late did not get in. The message got around. Soon the slaves began to pay closer attention to the clock.

Dr. White, like most Virginia pastors, had a regular midweek prayer meeting. In these services, he made it a point to call on one of the members to lead in prayer. Having approached the Major, he asked if he would be willing to pray publicly in one of these services.

"I-I'm not accustomed to speaking in public."stammered Jackson.

"You need not worry. The Lord will help you,"
encouraged White.

"Yes, but . . ." Jackson was gripped by a wave
of terror.

Dr. White laughed. "I, too, was afraid to speak
in public at first. I thought my legs would collapse
when I first stood behind a pulpit. But now public
speaking doesn't bother me."

Jackson swallowed hard. Forcing himself, he said,
"You are my pastor and the spiritual guide of the
church. If you think it my duty, I'll waive my
reluctance . . ."

After a few weeks, the pastor said, "And now Major
Jackson will lead us in prayer."

Although his heart was racing even faster than it
had at Chapultepec when the bullets were splattering
around him, Jackson slowly got to his feet. He
stumbled over each word. And it seemed that the
harder he tried, the more mixed up he became. After
what seemed an eternity, he managed a faint "amen"
and collapsed into his pew. He was embarrassed and
so was the pastor and the entire congregation.

Mercifully, Dr. White did not ask him to pray again
for a long time. Although Jackson was thankful, he
was disturbed. Upon meeting the pastor during an
early morning walk, he brought up the subject.

"I don't want to cause you any more discomfort,"
explained White.

"Yes," replied Jackson, "but my comfort or
discomfort is not the question; if it is my duty to lead
the brethren in prayer, then I must persevere in it,
until I learn to do it aright."

Within a week or two Dr. White called upon him
again. This time, he did better. Eventually, he became
so fluent the members looked forward to his public
prayers.

Public praying in church was not Jackson's only difficulty. Another was that he found it difficult to stay awake. Try as he would his eyes eventually got heavy and he would begin to nod. His friends explained that the problem was dyspepsia.

Once, after he had dozed in church, Margaret Junkin, the oldest daughter of Dr. George Junkin, president of Lexington's Washington College, approached with a suggestion. "Major Jackson," she said in the kindest voice she could manage, "you should not sit up so straight in church. If you were to lean back a little, when you nod off to sleep, it wouldn't be so noticeable."

Jackson replied with his usual logic: "I will do nothing to superinduce sleep by putting myself at ease, or making myself more comfortable; if, however, in spite of my resistance I yield to my infirmity, then I deserve to be laughed at, and accept as punishment the mortification I feel."

Going to sleep in church was not Jackson's only problem. Another was that he was not a good teacher; and, moreover, he knew it. But, he firmly believed that God had called him to V.M.I. and if God had called him, he reasoned, He would enable him to become effective.

In order to teach better, he tried to sit up late at night so that he could master his material. But since his eyes were failing, this became impossible. He then devised a unique system. He used every spare moment of daylight to read. Then at night, after his evening meal, he went into strict seclusion and mentally went over his subject point by point. By using this method, he was enabled to teach without manuscript.

Determined as he was, he mastered—and taught!—calculus, and other forms of higher mathematics. Still, his main interest remained in artillery, and his great hero in that subject was Napoleon Bonaparte, the little Corsican who had nearly conquered all of Europe.

But in spite of his busy life, Jackson was frequently discouraged. Then one day after church he met another daughter of Dr. Junkin, Margaret's sister, Elinor. Clear-eyed Elinor was twenty-six, just a year younger than himself. She was a devout Christian and had beautiful dark hair which she parted in the center and swept back over her ears. Suddenly, Major Jackson, hero of Chapultepec, discovered that he was in love. Viewing himself in the mirror, he smiled. It was a wonderful feeling to be in love. Meeting Elinor had changed everything!

13

Agony Of Loving And Losing

As meticulous in love as he was with artillery, Jackson determined to learn all about the Junkins before he launched his campaign to win Elinor.

Dr. George Junkin, he learned, was born in Pennsylvania of Scotch-Irish parents. He had become a minister in the Associate Reformed Church, a denomination that resembled the Presbyterians. Julia Rush Miller, his wife, also came from a fine family.

Challenged by the need for more schools, Dr. Junkin helped to found Lafayette College in Easton, Pennsylvania; had been the president of Miami University in Oxford, Ohio—and in 1848 had assumed the presidency of Washington College in Lexington.

The Junkins were the parents of eight children.

Jackson liked what he had learned; but he was a little worried because Junkin was rather austere—and determined. As he shook the president's hand for the first time, he wondered about his opinions concerning slavery. Since he had lived in Ohio, would he side with the North or with the South if war broke out between the two sections?

Concerned about whether or not he was *really* in love, Jackson called on his respected friend, Major Hill, whom he had met in Mexico. Hill had helped him with his doctrinal difficulties. Perhaps, like a doctor with a stethoscope, he would tell him whether or not he was in love, or merely infatuated.

After a long conversation, during which Jackson kept referring to Elinor and finally blushingly confessed, "I used to think her plain, but her face now seems . . . all sweetness." Hill burst out laughing. "You *are* in love," he announced with the certainty of a medical specialist. "Yes, you are in love. There is no doubt about it. You have all the symptoms!"

Having concluded that the Junkins had excellent roots, were fine Christians, and that he was not merely infatuated but had lost his heart, he carefully planned a campaign that would make Dr. Junkin his father-in-law.

Soon, he began to sit with Elinor in church; then he took her out to dinner. Finally, her mother, Julia, invited him to have dinner with them.

Jackson carefully prepared for his first entrance into the Junkin home. He made certain that his hair and sideburns were just right, that his boots glistened, and that his clothes were immaculate.

Before leaving his room, he prayed that God would have His way in his life.

Jackson walked over to the president's red brick house on College Hill, and timidly knocked. "Dinner isn't quite ready," said Dr. Junkin, after inviting him in and indicating a chair. While they waited, Jackson noticed a copy of *Uncle Tom's Cabin* on an end table.

"What do you think of that book?" he ventured.

Junkin smiled. "It's a spellbinder, and it's getting people all stirred up. I couldn't lay it down."

"Some have said that Harriet Beecher Stowe knows very little about slavery. Do you believe that?" Jackson studied him carefully.

"True, she was only in the South over a weekend; but living in Cincinnati, right across from Kentucky, she came in daily contact with slavery. Her brother Henry Ward even helped a slave escape on the underground railway."

"Doesn't she show slavery at its very worst?" asked Jackson.

"That she does. But she had to use a little melodrama in order to reach the public. Actually, President Fillmore's Fugitive Slave Law will stir up more animosity than a dozen *Uncle Tom's Cabins*."

"What do you mean?"

"According to that law anyone can accuse any black of being a fugitive slave. Moreover, the accused is not allowed to testify in his own behalf, and—get this— if the judge determines that the black is guilty, he is paid $10, but if he proclaims him innocent, he only gets $5."

"But hasn't the law eased tensions between the North and the South?" asked Jackson.

Junkin just started to answer when dinner was announced. "We'll talk about it later," he said, motioning toward the dining room.

The table was crowded by a large ham, a platter of turkey, mashed potatoes, gravy, and three or four other vegetables. After grace, the conversation got stuck in small talk. Jackson was conscious that they were evaluating him. But he didn't mind, for Elinor was dressed in her finest, and by her smiles and tone of voice, he knew that he had at least met with her approval.

The Major and Elinor continued to see one another. Their hand-in-hand walks became longer, his gifts became more expensive, and he was invited to the Junkin home more frequently. Then suddenly, like a clap of thunder, their romance was over. Horrified, Jackson tried to arrange another date. Elinor said, "No!" and she would even pass him on the street without a wave. At the end of three months, he was so discouraged he told Major Hill that he was thinking of becoming a missionary, and hoped that he would die on a foreign field.

Unable to stand the pressure, he eventually went to the Hills' home one night at midnight, pounded on the door to awaken them, and demanded that Mrs. Hill go over to the Junkins' and act as a go-between.

"I-I c-can't go t-tonight," stuttered Julia Hill as she pulled her dressing gown close, "but I will go over and see her tomorrow."

Speaking confidentially, Major Hill asked Jackson about some of his odd mannerisms. Why did he suck on lemons so often? "It helps my dyspepsia," answered Jackson. Why did he sometimes stretch out his right arm at shoulder height while walking along the street? "Because I'm convinced that I'm not properly balanced. By doing that, I help restore balance in my body."

"Mmmm. Have you told the Junkins about your experiences in Mexico?"

"No. I don't like to brag."

"Well, if I were you I'd do just that. After all, you *were* the hero at Chapultepec!"

Jackson shrugged. "I like to be modest."

"Nonsense!"

Mrs. Hill did go over to the Junkins, and she did get the two back together. The Major followed his friend's advice about his Mexico experiences, and he tried to explain to Elinor about some of his mannerisms, and after a time the problems in their relationship unraveled.

Soon Tom Jackson and Elinor were engaged, but the Junkins insisted their engagement remain a secret. Tom complied, not even mentioning it to his sister Laura.

Jackson continued to visit the Junkin home. There, he and the Doctor often spent hours discussing the tensions between the North and the South.

"The Missouri Compromise was a move in the right direction," said Junkin, over a cup of tea.

"Why do you think so?" asked Jackson. "I'm a military man. Please explain."

"It was like this. In 1818, after the Missouri Territory had been carved out of the Louisiana Purchase, Missouri applied to become a part of the Union. Missouri had 3,000 slaves, so if Missouri were to become part of the Union, slave states would have two more senators than the free states. The free northern states didn't like that at all!'' Junkin continued, as he filled both his and Jackson's cups. ''Finally, it was decided that the southern boundary of Missouri would become the dividing line between slave states and free states. But the natives of Missouri then drew up their constitution and put in two clauses that the free states didn't like.''

''What were the clauses?'' asked Jackson.

''One was that no freed Negro could even enter Missouri. The other, that no Missouri slave could be freed without his master's consent.''

''So now what's going to happen?'' asked Jackson as he set down his teacup.

Junkin held up his hands. ''Only God knows!'' He shook his head.

''A year before you came,'' he continued, ''The compromise of 1850 was passed. As you know, the Compromise gave Texas $10,000,000 for their claims against the territory of New Mexico—then to satisfy the North, the District of Columbia was declared free.''

Jackson became so absorbed he couldn't take his eyes away from Dr. Junkin.

''Didn't California enter the Union as a free state?'' he asked.

''Yes it did, and to further complicate matters, the territories of New Mexico, Utah and Arizona may decide whether *they* will be free or slave states!''

Junkin stood up. ''Ah, but I'd better go to my office.''

He paused at the door long enough to say. ''Right now, the Missouri Supreme Court is deciding the case of one *Dred Scott*, a slave owned by a doctor in Missouri. The doctor took this slave to the free state

of Illinois, then to Wisconsin. When he returned to
Missouri, he sold him to another—and then left the
state. The slave—Scott—thought that he might be free
because he had lived in free states, so he sued for his
freedom. The St. Louis County Court decided Scott
was free; the Missouri Supreme Court reversed that
decision; now it has been taken to the United States
Supreme Court. Their decision could be very
significant.''

''You mean their decision might be a step toward
a war between the states?'' Jackson stood up.

''Perhaps.''

Jackson was a little disturbed about the expanding
atmosphere of war, but he was in love. Right now,
romance seemed more important than a potential war
between the States.

During the morning of August 4th, Major Jackson
casually stopped at the Hills', teased Anna and
Eugenia Morrison, Mrs. Hill's attractive sisters, both
in their twenties, then with a glance at his watch,
remarked, ''I think I'd better be going.'' He put on
his hat, pulling the front brim downward toward his
nose as was his habit, and began to suck a lemon, then
he headed for the red brick Junkin home on College
Hill. On the way, he passed a number of cadets. None
knew why his step was so firm.

Upon entering the parlor, he was joined by Elinor.
There, Dr. George Junkin asked them the usual
questions, led in prayer—and formally announced that
they were man and wife.

The wedding trip had been carefully planned. The
happy couple headed for Philadelphia, and then West
Point. Jackson took Elinor to Canada and told her
the story of how the French had wanted to establish
a foothold in Quebec. But in 1759 the British decided

to capture Quebec and make it a British stronghold.
"If General Wolfe had not conquered Quebec and
made Canada British," said Jackson, "you and I
might be subjects of Queen Victoria."

"Oh?" questioned Elinor.

"If Wolfe had not conquered Quebec, and made
Canada British, King George would have been more
diplomatic with the Colonies, and they would have
remained a part of his empire."

One day the Jacksons were taken on a tour to the
plains of Abraham, where there was a monument
constructed in honor of British General Wolfe.
Emotionally, Jackson told his wife more details of the
General's life. Then he said, "Ellie, listen while I read
Wolfe's last three words: Enunciating clearly, he read:
"*I DIE CONTENT.*" Then holding his wife close he
asked: "To die as *he* died, who would not be content?"

Their honeymoon over, the Jacksons moved into
the Junkin home, where they occupied nearly an entire wing.

Due to the death of the professor of mathematics
at the University of Virginia, a replacement was
needed. Jackson applied. Colonel Robert E. Lee
recommended him.

After proudly showing the letter to Elinor, he
exclaimed: "Listen to what the Colonel wrote: 'His
conduct while at the Acad'y was in every way
exemplary.'" He refolded the letter, then after kissing her, he all but shouted, "We're in Ellie!"

Other letters followed. All were strongly in his favor.
But the University's board of Visitors, preferred
Albert Taylor Bledsoe, a mathematician who was
fifteen years older than Jackson, and who had
considerably more experience.

The Jacksons were disappointed. Then, while the

were still feeling the disappointment, Elinor's mother became seriously ill. The doctors admitted they were unable to save her life—stating that there was nothing more they could do.

Knowing she would soon be gone, Julia summoned the children to her bedside and exhorted them to be "kind to one another and to love Jesus."

Shortly after her mother's funeral, Elinor brightened the atmosphere by announcing to Tom that she was expecting a baby. "Wonderful!" he cried. "About when will it be due?"

"In October."

The always gentle Major became even more compassionate. Daily after classes, he and Ellie daydreamed together. They discussed names, purchased a crib, bought all the necessities.

Tragically, the baby was stillborn. A few days later, Elinor passed away. Tom and Ellie had been married fourteen months. Three deaths in less than a year were devastating!

All but crushed, Jackson grew more and more dependent on God's Word for comfort and the will to go on. To friends he wrote, "From my heart I thank God that though He has left me to mourn. . . He has taken dear Ellie to Himself. Her companions are of the Glorified Host, and I look forward with delight to the day when I shall join her."

Ellie was buried next to her mother in a Lexington cemetery at the top of the hill near where Main Street continued on toward the Natural Bridge. Day after day Jackson made his way to their graves to pay his respect and to draw close to the Lord.

Gradually, as Jackson was regaining his composure. friends persuaded him that he should vacation in Europe. Having longed to visit Waterloo, he finally agreed. He sailed on the steamship *Asia* for Liverpool

on July 9, 1856. Leaning against the rail as the
shoreline disappeared, he prayed that when he
returned from his vacation he would have renewed
vitality for the years ahead.

14

Thunder Rumbles

On board the ship sailing toward Liverpool, Jackson started thinking of Anna Morrison, a sister of Mrs. Hill. He had met both Anna and her sister, Eugenia, even before he married Elinor Junkin. He had liked them both, and often arranged escorts to take them to church. On occasion, he, himself escorted Anna. At that time, Anna was twenty-two, which meant that she was now twenty-five.

He also remembered how he had teased them the afternoon of his wedding and how Anna had blushed. Both were full of fun. As he reminisced, he decided that the always vivacious Anna was the prettier sister. Better yet, she knew how to laugh!

But he shook the memories from his mind and immersed himself in a new biography of Napoleon. Then he glanced at his itinerary which indicated that he would view some of England's finest cathedrals, then head for Scotland.

He checked to see when he would visit Waterloo, the most coveted spot in his journey; and he prepared himself by once again reading the details of how the little man in the green uniform fought, and lost, that battle.

Finally he arrived in Belgium, and ten miles southeast of Brussels he stepped onto the field of Waterloo where the battle that changed the map of Europe had been fought.

Details which had lain dormant in Jackson's mind leaped into plain view as he walked around.

Napoleon, the undisputed master of artillery, had been certain that he would defeat Wellington without much trouble. Wellington had many untried troops. *His* were veterans. Wellington had 159 cannon; Napoleon had 240 cannon. In addition, just two days before, he had forced the Redcoats to retreat at Quatre Bras. That defeat had undoubtedly demoralized them.

At dawn, two days later, Napoleon faced two major problems: An all-night rain had so thoroughly muddied the plains of Waterloo it was almost impossible to move his cannon; and the Prussians under Blücher could be expected to show up in the afternoon and aid Wellington. The key to victory, Napoleon knew, was to defeat Wellington before the Prussians could get there.

Jackson's thoughts spun in his mind as he stood and gazed. Napoleon tried to wait for the mud to harden before he could order his men to start the battle. The sun rose, but the field remained sloppy with mud. However, Napoleon grew desperate because he feared Blücher was on the way, so he reluctantly issued the order to start firing.

He then faced another problem. When the cannon balls reached their targets, instead of spreading deadly grape, they sank into the mud and merely produced volcanoes. Even so, it seemed that Wellington was retreating. Excitedly, Napoleon sent word to Paris that the battle had been won.

Completely confident that one massive blow was all that was needed, he rose in his stirrups and ordered Milhaud and his cavalry to charge and crush Wellington whom, he was convinced, was in a depressed area just beyond his view.

Milhoud's cavalry was made up of 3500 massive men mounted on choice, specially trained horses. Anxious to be the final blow that would defeat Wellington, the men lunged forward. As they advanced, the bands played, and the horsemen with their sabers drawn, shouted as one voice *Vive l'empereur!*

Jackson pondered this event and visibly shuddered; for he had often studied the disaster that followed. Unknown to Napoleon or the charging men, a ditch twelve feet deep stretched in front of them. It was the road to Ohain. Unable to stop, the first wave of horsemen plunged into the ditch, and the next wave and following waves piled on top of them.

Turning away from the field, Jackson remembered that as the sun neared its horizon, Blücher and his Prussians showed up. Napoleon was utterly defeated.

After four months of travel, Jackson boarded ship for his return to America. Day after day as he stood at the rail or relaxed with Napoleon's biography in his hands, two thoughts kept haunting his mind. One concerned Napoleon and that hidden ditch. *Why hadn't he known about it?* Obviously he could not have seen it through his spyglass, for it was extremely abrupt. *But why hadn't he ordered the area surveyed by a spy or an advance guard?* The professors at West Point had emphasized that this should always be done. Always! The truth, he discovered later, was that the guide Lacoste had not noticed the ditch, and had reported that the way was clear. Ah, but the guide should have known, for a white chapel stood at the crossroad where the road in the ditch made a junction with the Nivelles road! Perhaps if he had been accustomed to paying more attention to the word of the Lord, he would not have overlooked the ditch.

Mulling over Waterloo, Jackson became even more convinced that God is sovereign, and that in the end He always has His way.

Anna Morrison also slipped into his mind. He wondered where she was, what she was doing—and whether or not she was still single. Secretly, he wished he had her portrait. Praying about it, he determined that he would make contact with her as soon as he returned home.

Since the Major didn't reach Lexington until October, he was late for the opening of school. "You're always so punctual," teased Maggie Junkin. "What happened? Have you forgotten that professors, especially military professors, should never be late? Doesn't it bother your conscience?"

"Not at all," replied Jackson, faking an offended look. "I did all in my power to be here on time; but when the steamer was delayed by Providence, my responsibility was at an end."

Memories of Anna Morrison crowded out any guilt feelings he might have had about being late. He had not seen her since his marriage three years before. *Were his memories of her correct?* There was one certain way to find out. After putting on his hat, and selecting a piece of lemon, he marched over to the Hill house.

"I-I haven't called on y-you since I left," he mumbled to Mrs. Hill at the door. "You must remember that you befriended me once by mending my romance with Elinor." He forced a laugh.

"That I did. The silly girl just didn't understand you."

"While I was gone I sometimes thought about your sister Anna." He sank into an upholstered chair in the parlor.

"Anna is a sweet girl." Mrs. Hill smiled.

"Y-Yes I know. How—uh—is she getting along?"

"Oh, fine."

"Would you happen to have her address? I'd like to s-s-send her a brief note."

"That would be very kind of you." Mrs. Hill's smile widened.

"Of course I wouldn't want to write to her if she's married." He bit his lip and tried to keep his head high, but couldn't quite manage it.

"Oh, she's still single."

"She is?" Jackson's eyes widened and his jaw sagged.

"As far as I know, she is."

"Then give me her address!" He spoke with emphasis as if he were drilling troops.

After folding the slip of paper and storing it in his pocket, Jackson excused himself and headed for his apartment. He had longed to see a picture of Anna, but had lacked the courage to ask.

In his first letter to Anna, he reviewed the summer of 1853 when he had met her and taken her to church; and then slyly mentioned how lonely he had been, especially on his European trip.

Unable to suppress his ardor, Jackson headed for Charlotte, North Carolina in the middle of December.

When he arrived dressed in his finest blue uniform made even more splendid by its long rows of brass buttons, he stepped out of his carriage, climbed the high steps to the porch, and knocked at the door.

The Morrisons were delighted to see him. They led him into their library. As they visited, Jackson sensed that they were happy that he had come; and that they

were especially pleased to know that he was a devout
Christian.

When the atmosphere became a little awkward,
Doctor Morrison smiled and said, "Perhaps you and
Anna would like to visit with one another in the
parlor."

Without answering, both Anna and Jackson stood;
and Anna led the way through the nearby door.

They were sitting opposite each other in the
beautifully furnished room, when Anna suddenly
exclaimed, "Oh, it's cold in here! Excuse me while
I ask a servant to build a fire."

The servant built the fire, but it soon went out.
Then he built another which also flamed but for a
moment. After the third attempt failed, Anna
shrugged and said, "Maybe we'd better return to the
library. I'd hate for you to catch a cold."

Jackson noted with pleasure that there was a touch
of reluctance in her voice.

When they returned to the library, the Morrisons
excused themselves, and the Doctor said, "I'll have
to see why a fire doesn't burn in that fireplace. This
is the first time it has ever caused trouble." Morrison
discovered that some brick had fallen loose and
blocked the draft.

Meanwhile, Tom and Anna continued in
conversation and after that night, they announced
their engagement. They planned to be married at Cottage Home the following July. The days snail-paced
along, but Jackson sent a special letter every Monday. One letter said:

> When in prayer for you last Sabbath, the tears
> came to my eyes, and I realized an unusual degree
> of emotional tenderness....I felt as if it were
> communion day for myself.

While the Major and Anna continued their courtship by mail, the entire nation seethed with speculation as to what decision the Supreme Court would make in the Dred Scott case. Northerners, especially abolitionists, were afraid that the Supreme Court might declare the Missouri Compromise unconstitutional. If such a decision were made, it was widely believed that the chances of war between the North and the South would be greatly increased.

Some hysterical people all but heard the clash of arms.

Living on edge, Jackson nervously followed newspaper stories about the case. It was brought before the Supreme Court during the previous February, but without decision. Then it was scheduled for more debate to start on February 15, 1857.

By this time, each shred of information about the problem became copy for reporters. Headlines were made by Justice Curtis of Massachusetts and Justice McLean of Ohio. Each declared that he would defend the constitutionality of the Missouri Compromise.

Although Jackson held his breath, he and Anna continued with their wedding plans. They agreed that the Reverend Doctor Lacy, president of Davidson College, was to perform the ceremony; and they agreed that when he asked the questions, he would address them by only their first names.

When the great day finally was upon them, the happy couple faced two formidable hazards. The first was that there was some uncertainty about the marriage license. According to North Carolina law, a $500 bond would have to be posted. There wasn't much time. What would they do? One of the wedding party, perhaps Doctor Morrison, leaped on a horse and rode furiously to Lincolnton, the county seat. The bond was eventually signed by William W. Morrison.

The next problem was even more dramatic! Anna's wedding dress ordered from New York had not arrived. "We must not take chances," said one of the group. "We'll make another ourselves. Soon Anna was being measured, and a seamstress got busy. While Anna watched the clock, her dress was rapidly stitched together. Then, just several hours before the wedding, the one from New York arrived. Since it was far better than the home-made one, Anna decided to wear it.

After the wedding, the Jacksons went on a long honeymoon. On their return, they moved into the Lexington hotel. Soon, the Major was besieged by health problems. He lost a great deal of his hearing in one ear, had to have his throat cauterized twice a week, and his eyes became worse. While these diseases were tormenting Jackson, the Chief Justice of the Supreme Court, Roger B. Taney, announced the decision, reached by a vote of six to two, that Dred Scott was still a slave. That decision was halfway expected by everyone, but it was also announced that the Missouri Compromise was, and had always been, unconstitutional. That added decision was like the explosion of a munitions factory. It rocked every state and all the territories.

Senator Jefferson Davis and most of the South were delighted, but the North responded with outbursts of rage. When Major Jackson saw the headlines, he gathered Anna into his arms, "The Union will be divided," he said. "*The thunder is rumbling!* Our nation is headed for war. Anna, we must pray!"

15

Lightning Strikes

Uncomfortable in the hotel, the newlyweds moved into a boarding house. This was better. But they still weren't satisfied. "I want a home of my own," said Anna. "And we'll need one soon. I'm expecting."

"You're expecting! When's it due?"

"At the end of April or the beginning of May."

"That's wonderful!" He pulled her onto his lap and kissed her again and again. "Let's go out and celebrate."

During the winter of 1858 they found an old house on Washington Street which they could afford. Anna was skeptical. The house needed so much work.

"It's only a block from the church and we can remodel it," assured the Major.

As they worked and planned, Anna began to complain about morning sickness. Jackson tried to reassure her.

As snows fell, the Jacksons mended walls, bought furniture and rugs, put up curtains—and used their paint brushes. They had barely finished when their daughter made her appearance on April 30, 1858. They named her Mary Graham in honor of her grandmother. But in less than a month, little Mary came down with what they considered to be yellow jaundice.

Mary died on May 25.

Heartbroken, Jackson wrote to Laura's daughter Grace:

> *Your sweet little cousin and my daughter was called from this world of sin to enjoy the heavenly happiness of Paradise.... While your Aunt Anna and myself feel our loss, yet we know that God has taken her away in love. Jesus says, "Suffer little children to come unto me, and forbid them not, for of such is the kingdom of heaven."*

The Jacksons became extra busy mending their hearts by prayer, improving their house—and in daily routine. Early at six, Tom arose by himself, sank to his knees, and had a quiet time with the Lord. Then, slanting the brim of his hat until it pointed toward his nose, and selecting a lemon, he went for a walk. Walks were important to him. He continued them in all sorts of weather. During these walks he maintained his habit of periodically holding out his right arm.

At seven he returned home, and had prayer with Anna and the servants. Then he had breakfast and marched off to school. Precisely at 11, he secluded himself in his private office. There he read his Bible, and studied the books he was teaching. *Analytical Mechanics* and *Optics and Acoustics* were difficult subjects. He wanted to be at his best.

Following this, he want home for dinner which was served at the moment the hour hand of the clock reached one, Jackson's routine was so exacting that citizens could set their clocks by what he was doing. These eccentric ways inspired many to laugh behind their hands. Still, everyone respected his unbelievable honesty. Having learned that he had misinformed a professor about a cadet, he trudged through a rainstorm in order to set things right, even though he could have made his explanation the following morning.

Convinced that Amy, an elderly slave, was being mistreated, he, at her request, bought her; and after he married Anna, she became their cook. In 1859 Jackson bought an eighteen-acre farm. He bought more slaves to work on his farm and his house. All of his slaves were expected to attend his family worship. He was strict. Should one of them go through a door without closing it, he often waited until the slave was on another floor or across the house, then he called, "You forgot to close the door!"

Owning slaves in Lexington was commonplace. Even the preachers owned slaves. On the whole, they were treated well; and seldom were families broken up by having a member sold to another master. As always, there were exceptions.

Anna's favorite slave was Hetty who had helped at the birth of Mary. Hetty had two sons: Cyrus who was twleve and George who was sixteen. Anna taught both to read, and the Major drilled them in Bible doctrine.

Tensions between the North and South continued to sharpen. The possibility that war might break out between the states was accepted and dreaded by everyone. The word *secession* became familiar, especially in the South. Also, heated discussions sprang up about "states' rights." Many claimed to be *statriots* rather than patriots.

Union Street in Charleston was renamed State Street.

There were extremists in both the North and the

South. John Brown, Jr., was one of these. The Jacksons read all they could about this tall, bearded, fierce-looking man.

Father of twenty children, John Brown lived in Kansas where conflicts over slavery were at white-heat. He was a never-give-in abolitionist, claiming that he had been divinely directed to fight the slave-masters and to free their slaves.

He became an expert hit-and-run fighter. When he massacred a band of proslavery men from Missouri at Osawatomie, the South denounced him as a criminal and the North praised him as a mistaken but courageous zealot.

Inspired by the headlines, Brown decided that by a bold move he would free all the slaves. On October 16, together with about 20 followers, he seized the Federal arsenal at Harpers Ferry, Virginia. Convinced that slaves all over the country would revolt if he dared to lead the way, he planned to take a few hostages in the town and hold them to exchange for slaves.

At first the citizens of Harpers Ferry were so stunned, he managed to seize a few. But the towns-people soon rallied and surrounded the arsenal. During the fracas, a Negro was killed by one of Brown's men, and several others were wounded.

A day or two later, United States troops under the command of Colonel Robert E. Lee, surrounded the arsenal and Brown, along with his men were taken into custody.

"What do you think they'll do to him?" asked Anna.

"He'll have a speedy trial and will be hanged," replied the Major. He folded the paper and placed it on the table. "But the Union will be torn apart, and there will be war between the states."

The jury only required forty-five minutes to declare

Brown guilty of murder, and he was sentenced to hang. The Governor of Virginia worried that there might be an outbreak of violence at the public scaffold. He therefore ordered the Corps of Cadets at Virginia Military Institute to be present at Charleston for the hanging. Dressed in full uniform, Major Jackson accompanied them. He was to command the artillery.

On that fateful day, between 8 and 9 a.m. the cadets marched to the little hill where the scaffold had been erected. Jackson took care of a howitzer he had placed on the right. Lieutenant Trueheart was in charge of one on the left.

Each cadet had a cartridge box containing twelve rounds of ball cartridges. Long before the trap was scheduled to be sprung, the cadets were ordered to lie down facing the gallows with their guns ready beside them.

Jackson's eyes swept the line where his well-trained "boys" were stationed, and he noticed an unusual character whom he learned was sixty-six-year-old Edmund Ruffin, a dedicated Secessionist. He had borrowed a uniform and spent the night with the cadets in order to have a *better view* of the hanging.

Among the guards, stood another unusual character—an actor by the name of John Wilkes Booth.

About 11 a.m. three companies of heavily-armed militia crossed the field. Then came a wagon drawn by two white horses.

Straining, Jackson noticed that John Brown was sitting on a black coffin. He was dressed in black. His arms were tied behind him, and he ascended the scaffold with apparent cheerfulness.

As the hangman lifted an ax to sever the rope which held the platform on which Brown was standing, Jackson sent up a petition that his soul might be saved.

Awful was the thought that he might die without the Lord. But Jackson knew that Brown had refused to have a minister with him the evening before.

At this very time, city officials in Albany, New York, were firing a one hundred gun salute in honor of the "martyr." Church bells from New England to Kansas tolled for him. After his funeral people began singing a new song to a lively camp meeting tune:

John Brown's body lies a-moldering in the grave,
His soul goes marching on.

Following the execution, Jackson was ordered to take his cadets to Richmond. There he drilled them in Capitol Square. Spectators cheered, but many had wistful looks in their eyes. Jackson, too, was disturbed. *Was he rehearsing for a war that was about to break out between the North and the South?* The thought sickened him. Then he remembered that he had gone all day without sucking a lemon.

Upon his return to Lexington, Anna threw her arms around him, and they talked about the nation's problems. "I believe in the Union," said Jackson, "but I also believe that slavery will end—in time. A disease has to run its course."

"Do you think *our* slaves would like to be free?" asked Anna.

"I'm not sure. What would happen if I gave them their freedom? What would they do and where would they live? Do you think Hetty and her sons would like to be left to survive on their own?"

"I-I don't know."

Anna was not feeling well, and after consulting with doctors the Major took her to Vermont where she could enjoy one of the famous hot mineral baths. The baths didn't help so he transferred her to the "Round Hill Water Cure" in Massachusetts. The doctor said she could be completely cured if she stayed until October, so Jackson returned to Lexington. The multi-storied house on Washington Street was lonely without Anna.

Far-reaching events were stirring the world but Jackson did not want to excite Anna with them. He specialized in writing to her about trivial things. He mentioned that he had buried ninety-nine heads of her cabbage for winter use, that he had watered her flowers, and that Hetty had canned many jars of plums and other fruit.

One event he didn't write about was the fact that after John Brown's execution, the Virginia Legislature decreed that the cadets at Virginia Military Institute were in the service of the State under military command. The professors had their salaries increased to $1800 a year, with the promise of an additional $100 every five years. The Major didn't have to ponder over the meaning of this, for the Legislature also earmarked half a million dollars for both the manufacture and purchase of arms. War clouds, he knew, were darkening.

Jackson called on his pastor. "Doctor White," he said, "would it not be worthwhile for the entire congregation to have a special prayer session and pray for peace?" The pastor agreed.

Southerners were becoming stirred up because it appeared that Abraham Lincoln would be nominated by the Republicans in their upcoming Chicago convention. They remembered his recent Cooper Union speech in which he said that none of the Founding Fathers had ever declared that the Federal Government should not have the power to control slavery in the territories. "I defy any man," he said, "to show that any one of them ever in his whole life declared that."

They also remembered a former campaign speech in which Lincoln had said, "A house divided against itself cannot stand. I believe this government cannot endure permanently half slave and half free. I do not expect the house to fall—but I do expect it will cease to be divided."

The South hoped that Lincoln would not be nominated; and, if he were, that he would be soundly defeated at the polls.

Jackson prayed earnestly that God would have His way.

16

Storm Rages

Even though spring was in the air and birds were singing, the atmosphere in Chicago's massive Wigwam was tense. Republicans should have been delighted because the Democrats were so divided that they had failed to nominate a candidate at their convention, and the opposing sides were planning separate conventions in June at which rival candidates would be nominated. This split all but guaranteed the election of a Republican.

But the Republicans were frustrated because they also seemed divided. Votes on the third ballot were counted, and they still had failed to nominate a candidate. Lincoln had 231 and a half votes, which was two votes less than he needed for victory.

Should there be a fourth ballot?

As the chairman pondered, heavily pocked David Carter from Ohio scrambled onto a chair. "O-Ohio," he stammered, "has s-s-switched four votes from Chase to Lincoln."

That switch to Lincoln was like a jolt of lightning.
Delegates became hysterical. Judge Stephen Logan
was so beside himself, he leaped onto a table and
began to yell and swing his arms. Forgetting his
normal dignity, he slammed his hat onto the head of
the man next to him with such force it was squashed
flat.

When the news reached Virginia, Jackson and his
wife were disturbed. "Do you think Lincoln can win
the election?" she asked over the breakfast table. Her
face was almost haggard with concern.

"He won't carry a single southern state, but many
in the North love him. He's a great story teller. The
outcome will depend on whom the Democrats
nominate."

During the turmoil, the Democratic party had
another split with the result that the three sections had
three candidates: John C. Breckenridge of Kentucky,
Stephen A Douglas of Illinois, and John Bell of
Tennessee.

The campaign was bitter. Lincoln was ridiculed.
It was claimed that he was descended from a gorilla,
and that he was ignorant. But when the votes were
counted in November, Lincoln won with 180 electoral
votes, while Breckenridge trailed with 72, Bell, 39,
and Douglas only 12. Nonetheless, the combined
popular votes of his opponents, totaled 949,165 more
than he received.

"We are in troubled times," said Jackson, "and
things will get worse." He put his arm around Anna.
"Soon I'll be faced with many decisions. Let's kneel
and pray that God will have His way."

During the Christmas holidays South Carolina
seceded from the Union. The following weeks were
tense in both the North and the South. Each
newspaper brought news of fresh perils. Following

South Carolina's lead, Mississippi also seceded from the Union. Then Florida, Alabama, Georgia, and Louisiana did the same. In Texas, Sam Houston had been elected governor on a "Save the Union" platform. But many Texans were so anxious to leave the Union, they out-voted Houston and seceded on February 1. Feeling defeated and disgusted, Sam Houston retired into private life.

The states that withdrew from the Union established their own government in Montgomery, Alabama, on February 4. They named it The Confederate States of America and elected Jefferson Davis of Mississippi President and Alexander Stevens of Georgia Vice President.

Later, Tennessee, North Carolina, Arkansas, and Virginia also joined them. Thus, the Confederacy was composed of eleven states. Most of these states were determined to maintain their independence from the North, even if they had to fight, but that feeling was not unanimous. In Tennessee, the vote to join the Confederacy was 105,000 to 47,000. In Virginia also, one-third of the voters, many in the western part, favored staying in the Union.

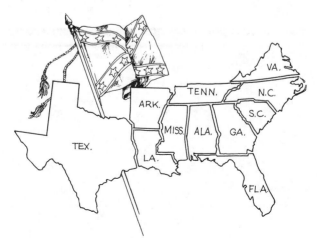

Both North and South feverishly prepared for war. The Confederacy seized Federal property: arsenals, post offices, ships. Alarmed, President Buchanan, who was still in in the White House, for Lincoln had not yet been inauguarated, proclaimed a fast day, and sadly confided to a friend that he was the last President of the entire United States.

A courageous chaplain opened the United States Congress by praying: "O Lord our God, we offer to Thee our humble praise for the past, the present, and for all the future. Will it please Thee for Christ's sake, to grant us Thy special aid? Thou knowest that our good men are at fault, and that our wise men are at fault; in the North and the South, in the East and in the West, they are at fault."

When Lincoln left Springfield for Washington on February 11, his route had to be changed because evidence of an assassination plot had been discovered.

In the midst of this nervous atmosphere, Major Robert Anderson, the commander of Fort Sumter in the harbor of Charleston, South Carolina, discovered that he was running low on supplies.

If President Lincoln ordered the Federal forces to withdraw, he would be accused of cowardice. If he forwarded supplies, the South might consider that an act of war. Caught between a rock and a hard place, Lincoln rushed supplies.

The Confederates considered this a hostile act, and their angry response was immediate. General Beauregard opened fire before dawn, at 4:30 a.m. The date was April 12, 1861. Curiously, the first shot was fired by Edward Ruffin, the Secessionist who had sneaked in with Jackson's cadets when John Brown was hanged.

On the evening of the 13th a group of slaves carried a flag of truce—a white handkerchief attached to the point of a saber, and rowed out to the fort. Fort Sumter surrendered at 7 p.m. No one on either side was killed during the bombardment. But when Major Anderson ordered his men to salute the flag as it was being lowered, a box of ammunition blew up and two men lost their lives.

News of the attack and surrender electrified the cadets at Virginia Military Institute. Fist fights erupted between the more rowdy ones and some citizens who favored the Union. The superintendent managed to herd the student body into a classroom and persuaded Jackson to speak to them. His speech was brief and to the point:

> *Military men make short speeches, and for myself I am no hand at speaking anyhow. The time for war has not come yet, but it will come and that soon, and when it does come, my advice is to to draw the sword and throw away the scabbard.*

On Monday, April 15, President Lincoln issued a call for 75,000 volunteers to suppress the rebellion.

Lincoln's call for volunteers was the final hammer blow that united the South, plunged the nation into war—and divided families.

Jackson's former father-in-law, Dr. George Junkin, was still president at Washington College. There, students had been flying a Confederate flag above the statue of George Washington on the highest part of the main building. Junkin ordered it removed. But when Lincoln issued his call, the students defiantly replaced it.

Again President Junkin ordered it lowered. But this time the faculty wholeheartedly agreed with the students, and it remained snapping in the breeze and defying the Union. Sick at heart, Junkin packed his things into a wagon. Accompanied by a niece and a daughter, he moved into Union territory. His daughter Maggie remained in Lexington.

"And what are *you* going to do?," asked Anna as she and Jackson watched Junkin's wagon pull out of the city.

"That's a hard decision." He held her tight.

"With whom does your sister Laura stand?"

"With the Union." A wry look twisted his face.

"Didn't you take an oath at West Point to uphold the Federal Government?"

"I did. But, Anna, Virginia is my home. I was born here. My parents were born here. If..." He spoke slowly and carefully, "If Virginia is invaded I have no choice but to be loyal to Virginia and the Confederacy."

On Saturday, April 20, word was received that VMI was on a war footing and that each cadet was in the army. The next morning at daybreak, Major Jackson received orders that he was to start marching the cadets to Richmond at 12:30.

"I hate to leave you, especially on Sunday," confessed the Major as he sat close to Anna. "But war is war, and orders are orders. I have no alternative..."

He left immediately for the Institute. After he had completed his final preparations, he hurried over to his pastor's study. "Doctor White," he began, "I've been ordered to take my cadets to Richmond. We'll be leaving at 12:30. Would it be possible for you to come over and give them a word of encouragement and pray with us?"

"I'll be there," replied the white-haired man.

Jackson hurried back home, had a quick breakfast, and then said to Anna, "Lets's have a moment of prayer before I leave." He turned to the 5th chapter of II Corinthians and began with the first verse: "*For we know that if our earthly house of this tabernacle were dissolved, we have a building of God, an house not made with hands, eternal in the heavens."*

By the time he had finished the chapter, both he and Anna were wiping their eyes.

When the pastor arrived, Jackson said, "Remember, we have to leave at exactly 12:30."

Doctor White smiled. "I'll be through at exactly 12:25," he promised.

The pastor finished on time just as he had said. But instead of moving, Jackson sat on a campstool. "Major Jackson, let's go!" urged a voice.

"It's not time yet." replied the blue-eyed deacon. Eyes on the clock, he waited until the minute hand touched 12:30. At that precise moment he barked: "Right face! By file, left march."

As the students marched out of Lexington their spirits zoomed. Many from their school, they believed, would become officers; and their cause, they felt assured, was worth every drop of blood they possessed. Invigorated by such thoughts, they obeyed Jackson's orders with precision and enthusiasm.

Just beyond Lexington they reached a column of wagons and stagecoaches that had been ordered to transport them to Staunton where they were scheduled to spend the night.

Late the next morning, the men were herded into the waiting train at Staunton which would take them to Richmond. As the wheels click-clacked over the rails, one of the cadets remarked, "The Yanks better beware. We're on our way and we're under the command of no other than Old Jack himself."

While passing through a tunnel in the Blue Ridge Mountains, the engine jumped the track. During the two hours required to repair it, Jackson wrote a note to Anna. Said he:

*Here , as well as at other points of the line, the war-spirit
is intense. The cars had scarcely stopped here before a request
was made that I leave a Cadet to drill a company . . . .*

The train reached Richmond after dark; and as the
men were disembarking, some were disappointed that
they had not been met with any fanfare. *After all, if
they were willing to give their lives for the Confederacy, should
not the citizens in the state capital show their appreciation?*

That the Confederates were unprepared for war
became evident to Jackson as he reviewed the
volunteers who had crowded into Richmond. Many
were barefoot. Some had brought the only weapons
they had: shotguns, smooth-bore muskets, pitchforks.

One day a total stranger approached. "Major
Jackson," he said without even saluting, "I've just
been made a corporal of the guard for the day, and
I haven't the slightest idea about what I'm to do."

Gritting his teeth, for Jackson surmised that the one
who had given the order probably didn't know any
more about procedures than the poorly clothed lad
himself, he led him around and gave him instructions.
"These are the sentry-posts," he said pointing to each
one. He also taught him salutes, the various
challenges, and the disciplines he was expected to
follow.

Jackson had reason to be discouraged. But when
he learned that Colonel Robert E. Lee, had been
named commander of the land and naval forces of
Virginia with the rank of Major General, he was
greatly encouraged.

17

There Stands Jackson!

Scores of Jackson's classmates at West Point were confronted with the decision about where they should serve. George B. McLennan didn't have a problem. Born in Pennsylvania, he had been reared a Union man. Others were not so fortunate.

Gustavus Smith, whose sympathies were with the Confederacy, was employed in New York City, and had sworn an oath to support the Union. However, he managed to "go South" in a unique, though dishonest way. He arranged to have an "acute" illness, and to have his "handsome coffin containing bricks...buried with honors." He then put on disguise, and slipped into Dixie.

He became a Major General.

Robert E. Lee's decision was most difficult and agonizing. Eight generations of Lees had lived in Virginia, and the state brimmed with cousins, aunts, uncles—and other relatives. He frowned on slavery, and he didn't believe in secession. What was he to do?

Being a realist, he knew that the Confederacy faced

a formidable and determined foe. The North, along with its seven territories, and 23 states, had a population of 23,000,000; while the South had only 11 states and a population of merely 9,000,000, and that number included 4,000,000 slaves—slaves who might not remain loyal. In addition, the North was far better equipped with factories, wealth—and a much larger navy.

One night, Lee's wife Mary, was kept awake by the sound of him pacing back and forth in an upstairs room. In the middle of the night, the pacing stopped. Mary knew then that Robert had made up his mind.

Having been the Superintendent at West Point, and possessing an excellent reputation for his character and engineering skills, Lee knew that he could go far with the Union. Moreover, he realized the peril his family faced since his home was in Arlington, Virginia, on the very fringe of the northern capital.

But in the depths of his being, he knew that he could never lift his sword against his native state. Having weighed his problems, he resigned his commission in the United States Army.

Upon hearing this news, the Governor of Virginia invited him to Richmond. There, he was offered the command of the Army of Virginia with the rank of Major General. After his acceptance, he lifted his hand and declared: "Trusting in Almighty God, an approving conscience, and the aid of my fellow citizens, I will devote myself to the defense and service of my native state, in whose behalf alone would I have ever drawn my sword."

He then donned the gray uniform of the South. That day he heard the new tune *Dixie* for the first time—and he liked it.

Virginia newspapers headlined the fact that the model soldier was now at the head of their forces. And as these headlines were read, over three hundred graduates of West Point began to head south. In their minds, Robert E. Lee and Pierre Beauregard were right.

The South manufactured guns, gathered troops, and sang "Dixie." They moved their capital from Montgomery, Alabama, to Richmond, Virginia.

This move was strategic, for everyone suspected that much of the fighting would be in Virginia. It was also an encouragement to the Upper South. And, since Washington D.C. was just a little over one hundred miles away, it showed defiance to the North. Also, Virginia was a great producer of grain, and their armies and horses would consume a lot of grain.

In like manner, the North prepared for the conflict. Old Fuss and Feathers was convinced that he *was* the man to lead the Union forces. He had won the Mexican War, had played a vital part in the War of 1812, and was still full of determination. In order to position himself to help, he wrote to Lincoln days before he arrived in Washington. Writing in the third person, in the manner of King George III, he said:

> Lieutenant-General Scott is highly gratified with the favorable opinion entertained of him by the president-elect, as he learns through Senators Baker and Cameron, also personal friends of General Scott.... The president-elect may rely with confidence on General Scott's utmost exertions in the service of his country....

While the newspapers argued about Scott, believers in the Union went around singing that although John Brown's body was a-moulderin' in the grave, "his soul goes marching on."

Old Fuss and Feathers was convinced that the best way to win the war was not by invading Virginia, his home state; but rather by controlling the Mississippi, and blockading all the eastern ports of the South.

The papers ridiculed his idea. A popular cartoon showed a snake coiled around the Confederacy and dubbed it, "Scott's Anaconda."

As both sides shuffled for the best position, Jackson received notice that he was now a Colonel and that he should take charge of the troops in Harper's Ferry which had just been evacuated by the North because they had decided that it was indefensible since it was at the bottom of a cone formed by rugged hills.

Having pulled the brim of his cap toward his nose and selected a lemon, Colonel Jackson went to work. His first order was to gather all the whisky barrels, knock the tops off, and pour the contents into the gutters. A few men knelt on the streets and cupped up all the whisky they could find.

Jackson announced that he would not tolerate drunkenness. Many grumbled and accused him of being a hard man. But they still respected him because he was fair. Moreover, all of them knew that he could be found in church every Sunday morning. Likewise, they knew that he usually slept during the sermon.

That spring, Jackson's men seized a Baltimore and Ohio train that contained a car filled with horses bound for the Federal Cavalry. Needing a horse, Jackson selected a large sorrel gelding—a neutered male. He liked its reddish-brown color and decided to keep it. Then he noticed a smaller gelding of the same color. This typical lady's horse would be ideal for his wife. He announced that he would take both.

Since the captured horses were booty; and thus, according to the rules of war, belonged to the Confederate Government, he mailed a check to Richmond for payment.

Jackson soon learned that the smaller horse was much easier to ride, so he allowed Chaplain Beverly

Tucker to use the big one. The little horse was so even
tempered and easy to ride, and so suited for a lady,
he named him Fancy. But to the men, the horses were
Big Sorrel and Little Sorrel.

Little Sorrel could never have won a beauty contest.
He measured about fourteen hands high, had lofty
withers; and, as he grew older, his back developed
a tendency to sway. But he had one great quality; he
could keep going day and night. This was a quality
Jackson especially appreciated. Sometimes he rode
him forty miles in a single day; and he was so fond
of the horse, he often fed him apples and other goodies
with his own hand.

General Lee's orders to Jackson were crisp. Since
Harper's Ferry was a Federal arsenal, the little town
on the confluence of the Potomac and Shenandoah
Rivers, and wedged in a gap of the Blue Ridge
Mountains, was considered a prize by both the North
and the South. Lee gave an order: ''It is desired that
you transfer the machinery to the Richmond
Armory.'' This machinery used to manufacture
muskets and rifles was important to the Confederacy,
for thousands of muskets and rifles were desperately
needed.

Convinced the Federals would soon attack to regain
this prized arsenal, Jackson drilled his men and
prepared for battle. But in the midst of his fevered
activity, General Joseph E. Johnson suddenly
appeared and handed him a letter.

Addressed to Colonel Jackson, the document stated:
''In obedience to the Secretary of War, the
undersigned assumes the command of the troops at
and in the vicinity of this place. Maj. E.E. McLean
will take the direction of the operations of the Quarter-
master's Department; Maj. W.H.C. Whiting of the
Engineer Corps.''

Jackson knew Johnson by reputation—he was a graduate of West Point, in the class of 1829—but since he had received no orders from either Governor Letcher or General Lee to surrender his command to another, he refused to comply. Instead, he replied in a letter that he would only give up his command if he received orders from Governor Letcher or General Lee.

Jackson's letter impressed Lee. It proved that his man from Clarksburg was determined to do that which is right. Jackson was therefore given the command of General Johnson's recently organized brigade. It consisted of a battery of artillery, together with five regiments of Virginia infantry.

Worried that Anna might misunderstand the fact that he had been replaced by General Johnson, he mailed a letter of assurance to her in North Carolina where she had moved in with her parents. Then, a week or two later, he sent another letter which concluded with, for him, a sugar-sweet sentence: "Little one, you are precious to somebody's heart! I have been greatly blessed by our kind Heavenly Father."

God's providence, he believed, was still shaping his life. How and why he did not know. He had faithfully followed Lee's orders. He remembered the letter he had written to him: "I have, in obedience to the orders of Governor Letcher, directed the rifle-factory machinery to be removed immediately." That, he knew, had been done. He had also kept a rifle factory busy in Harper's Ferry; and had produced, and shipped fifteen hundred rifles from Harper's Ferry.

His conscience was clear. He determined not to worry.

Soon after Johnson had assumed command, the Federals began to assemble in strength in order to retake the place. Since Johnson was certain that he could not deal with such overwhelming odds, he received permission to retreat. Before leaving, he burned the public buildings and blew up the railroad bridges that crossed the Potomac.

Soon after, Jackson was handed a letter from General Lee which was dated July 3., With widening eyes he read:

> *My dear general, I have the pleasure of sending you a commission of brigadier-general in the Provisional Army, and to feel you merit it. May your advancement increase your usefulness in the State.*

Jackson proudly forwarded Lee's letter to Anna, and in his personal letter commented: "I should be very ungrateful if I were not contented, and exceedingly thankful to our kind Heavenly Father."

Unknown to the Confederacy, Scott's Anaconda Plan was being ignored. "Why go to all that unnecessary trouble?" reasoned many. "Richmond is only a few marches away. Let's take Richmond! We can easily do that in ninety days."

On July 16, a mere thirteen days after Jackson's promotion, General McDowell headed an army of 30,000 as it marched to Manassas Junction, thirty miles southwest of Washington D.C. This rail center was the key to Richmond. Although he was heading the largest army that had ever been assembled on the North American continent, McDowell had been hesitant.

"We're not ready," he protested to his superior, General Winfield Scott.

Old Fuss and Feathers' reply was short and grim. Squaring his massive braid-loaded shoulders, he snapped: "You are green it is true, but the Confederates are green also; you are all green alike."

Another Union army under the command of General Robert Patterson patrolled the hills west of Manassas. His assignment was to keep the Army of Shenandoah from joining General Johnson, the one who had just retreated from Harper's Ferry. General Jackson's brigade was now a part of Johnson's army.

The Union commanders had great respect for Jackson. Many remembered how he had stood his ground at Chapultepec. They also realized that the Virginians understood the turns and twists and rivers in this country much better than they understood them. Nonetheless, most of the elite in Washington believed that the forthcoming battle would be a snap and the Confederate forces would soon be crushed. In this spirit, numerous high-ranking officials, together with their wives, planned to enjoy a picnic at Manassas. They prepared sandwiches and drinks in order to be ready when the guns began to fire. They also packed field glasses so that they could watch from a distance.

When Johnson received a note from General Beauregard that his army was needed to help him at Manassas, he, with Jackson's brigade in the lead, headed in that direction. Often at a double-quick, they waded the Shenandoah and ascended the Blue Ridge Mountains at Ashby's Gap. At 2 a.m. they paused for a few hours of rest at the village of Paris.

Here Jackson turned his men into a grove. "Lie down and get some rest," he told them. Not having had food or drink for many hours, they were soon asleep.

"Should we not post a guard?" asked an officer.

"No," replied Jackson, "let them sleep. I will personally guard them." As Jackson kept his eyes open, Little Sorrel lay down beside him, closed his eyes and went to sleep.

An hour before dawn, a member of Jackson's staff finally persuaded him to let him take his place. Jackson was soon asleep. But the moment a splinter of light entered the camp, the men were awakened and were on their way.

Jackson's brigade and Johnson's army reached Manassas Junction at four o'clock on Friday afternoon. There, they positioned themselves toward the center of Beauregard's army which was stretched in front of the Bull Run river. The Confederate defense line there was nearly eight miles long.

In the morning, as Jackson's men viewed the country, and noticed the many fresh graves, some of their spirits sagged. But Jackson lifted their morale by telling them that when the battle started and they charged the enemy, they should let go with their blood-curdling yell.

The men had practiced that yell weeks before. The *woh-who-ey* rose sharply in pitch on the *who* and then ended with a thud on the *ey*. This combination of Apache war whoop and wolf howl, mixed with the agonizing screams of a panther, had a terrifying effect. One victim confessed that when he heard it he felt as if a corkscrew were being screwed down the length of his spine.

Although there were feints and jabs here and there, the main Federal attack didn't come until early Sunday morning, July 21.

As cannon boomed, Jackson's brigade quivered in readiness. "Now we'll get 'em!" cried a former butcher.

It soon was apparent that Beauregard had positioned his men in the wrong place. The Confederate battle flag in hand, and ignoring the bullets whistling about him, Jackson paced back and forth. He was searching for an area where his men should take their stand. Soon, he noticed a plateau. Yes, that was *the* place! It provided a panorama of the entire battlefield.

His cannon facing the enemy, Jackson ordered his brigade to lie on their stomachs and be ready for action. At this point, a lone horse and rider from the Confederate front rode up fast toward them. The rider seemed full of fire. He had jet black eyes, long hair, and the uniform of a general officer.

"What troops are you and who is commanding?" he asked the first man he reached.

"We are five Virginia regiments who have just arrived," he was told. "General Jackson, over there, is our commander."

The strange officer then rode over to Jackson, whose staff crowded around to hear the news from the front. "I am General B.E. Bee, commanding South Carolina troops. We have been engaged all morning and have been overpowered. We will fall back on you for support. The enemy will make their appearance in a short time over the crest."

"Then sir," replied Jackson, "we will give them the bayonet!"

Rushing back to his men, Bee pointed and yelled with enthusiasm, "Look yonder! There are Jackson and his brigade standing like a stone wall. Let us determine to die here, and we will conquer. Rally behind them!"

The distant picnickers were in ecstasy. "The rebels are retreating! The rebels are retreating!" they shouted as they hugged one another. "We'll soon be in Richmond!"

But the spectators had rejoiced too soon. Their field glasses focused on the plateau, the picnickers forgot their sandwiches as in horror they saw line after line of Federals mowed down like blades of grass.

As his men fought, Jackson, with his left hand lifted high, moved back and forth and shouted encouragement. Suddenly he felt blood trickling down his arm. A quick examination showed that his middle finger had been struck.

"You'd better go to the rear," suggested a medic.

"Oh, it's just a scratch," replied Jackson. He continued to wave his men on.

The battle lines moved back and forth. At first it seemed the Confederates were winning; and then it seemed the Federals were winning. Guns spat death and the earth shook. General Bee fell, mortally wounded.

At a critical moment, after a Union flag was captured, Jackson spurred Little Sorrel into the center of his regiment, and shouted an order: "Reserve your fire until they come within fifty yards; then fire and give them the bayonet. And when you charge, yell like the furies."

Jackson's charge, accompanied by the rebel yell, was too much for the Federals. They broke rank, threw down their weapons, and fled.

Frightened, the picnickers scattered and hurried back to Washington. The statistics that followed them back to the capital, paled many faces—especially those in authority. They indicated the Union Army had lost vast quantities of equipment and 3000 men were killed, wounded, captured, or missing. General Jackson and his brigade were christened with the names, *Stonewall Jackson* and the *Stonewall Brigade*.

The Confederate losses were about 2000 killed.

As the surgeons were busy with the wounded, Dr. Hunter McGuire approached Jackson in order to examine his wound. "No, I can wait," he replied; "attend to the others first."

One doctor thought that Jackson's finger should be amputated. Jackson faced McGuire, "What's your opinion?"

"I'd try to keep it."

Jackson followed his advice.

A day after the battle, many in Lexington, curious to learn what had happened at Manassas, crowded the post office. Finding a letter from Jackson, Dr. White waved it in front of the throng. "Now we'll learn," he said. He slit it open and read:

My dear Pastor,
In my tent last night, after a fatiguing day's service, I remembered that I had failed to send you my contribution for our colored Sunday school. Enclosed, you will find my check for that object, which please asknowledge at your earliest convenience, and oblige yours faithfully.

"Didn't he mention the battle?" asked a tall man.

"No. I guess we'll have to learn that from the papers," replied White.

18

An "Encyclopedia Of Horrors"

Following the victory at Manassas, or Bull Run, General Jackson camped at Centreville about five miles north of the battlefield. There, he was on the very doorstep of Washington D.C. Three days after the battle, an officer visited his tent in order to learn if his wound was healing.

Finding him in the process of bathing his very swollen hand in a nearby stream, the officer had a question: "General, how is it that you keep so cool? You appeared to be utterly insensible to danger in the storm of shell and bullets which rained down upon you when your finger was hit?" The officer studied him curiously.

The newly christened Stonewall smiled. "Captain," he replied thoughtfully, "my religious belief teaches me to feel as safe in battle as in bed. God has fixed the time for my death. I do not concern myself about *that*, but to be always ready, no matter when it may overtake me."

Jackson glanced at his tent. Then, focusing his eyes onto those of the visitor, he added: "Captain, that is the way all men should live, and then all would be equally brave." The Captain felt that this was a subtle rebuke because of the way he had cursed during the battle. But he managed to merely swallow, as he forced a smile.

About two months after the Battle of Manassas, Anna journeyed from North Carolina for a visit. After kissing him, she snuggled up close and remarked: "I see, Stonewall, that you have a new name."

"And how do you like it?" He slanted his eyes and laughed.

"It's great, and it becomes you."

"Oh, but I'm not worthy of it."

"Didn't you turn the tide of battle?"

"I didn't. That credit belongs to the Lord—and to my brigade."

"You mean the Stonewall Brigade?"

Jackson shrugged. "I suppose so. They're brave and wonderful men. Even though half of them are barefoot and are dressed in rags, they never complain."

Glancing at his beard, she asked, "And what happened to that smooth chin you used to have?"

"Anna, I decided that I didn't have time to keep the sideburns trimmed, and so I'm lettin' 'em grow. I hope you like it."

"Of course I like it! I'm so proud of you." She kissed him again. "I heard that after the battle was over, Richmond celebrated by firing one hundred guns."

The Utterback family provided a room in their home for the Jacksons, and there they lived in much the same manner in which they had lived in

Lexington. Anna's stay was like a second honeymoon.

During the day, Anna watched as the troops drilled, ate with the officers, and sat with her husband in the prayer meetings and other services requested by Jackson and arranged by the chaplain. Dr. White preached morning and evening for five days. Other ministers also conducted services.

One fine morning as birds were singing, and herds of cattle were grazing, Stonewall led Anna over to the Manassas battlefield. Pointing, he said, "This is where General Bee used the word *Stonewall*. Somehow, that word and the tone of his voice put new life into his men. Unfortunately a Yankee bullet got him a moment later. He died in that stone house over there. It was being used as a hospital. General Bee was a fine man.

"But follow me," he continued. "I want to show you another interesting house. He secured a carriage and took her to a stone house near Manassas Junction close to the Bull Run river. While pointing at the magnificent home, he said: "That place belongs to Wilmer McLean. He made his fortune as a grocer in Alexandria. Before the battle, this area was occupied by our men. They were here to guard against an unexpected thrust by the Yanks.

"While McLean's cook was preparing dinner for General Beauregard and his staff, a Yankee shell fell down the chimney and exploded in the stew. It blew the stew all over the walls."

"And then?" Anna's eyes were wide.

"And then the cook had to prepare something else." Stonewall laughed and gave her an extra squeeze.

After a two-week stay, Anna had to return to North Carolina. Their parting was extremely sad, for they both realized the chances were they would never be in one another's arms again. Their final moments were spent in prayer.

That fall Jackson was promoted to the rank of major general. He was thankful, but he realized that bloody battles were ahead—battles in which tens of thousands would be killed, blinded, maimed. Often, as he knelt by his bed, he prayed for the boys on each side of the conflict. More than most, he realized that war is hell. And one of the saddest facts was that many of the boys were extremely young.

On the Union side, more that 2,000,000 were twenty-one or younger. Another million were less than eighteen. An additional 200,000 had not reached their sixteenth birthdays. 100,000 more were under fifteen. 300 were not quite thirteen; and twenty-five were merely ten or even less.

Most of the youngest ones were drummer boys.

The Confederate armies were also young, although perhaps not quite as young as the Northern armies. Added to this horror was the fact that many were related. Brothers fought brothers. Kentucky senator George B. Crittenden had two sons who became major generals. One was for the Union. The other was for the Confederacy.

During the Battle of Manassas, two wounded men were placed side by side in a stable which served as a hospital. One wore blue; the other gray. One was Henry Hubbard, the other was Frederick Hubbard. They hadn't seen each other for seven years.

At the siege of Vicksburg, thirty-nine regiments hailed from Missouri. Twenty-two were for the Stars and Stripes. Seventeen were for the Stars and Bars.

Mary Lincoln had three brothers who were killed fighting for the Confederacy.

Both armies had efficient systems for killing one another. Some muskets had smooth bores and were thus inefficient. But others had rifling that made the bullets spin, and were effective for hundreds of yards. The Union had two regiments of sharpshooters totaling 2,000 men. Dressed in forest green, they were crack shots.

To be accepted, a candidate was required to place ten shots, one after the other, in a ten-inch target at 200 yards. A favorite weapon was the .45-caliber James Target Rifle. It weighed fourteen pounds and was accurate up to 500 yards. Sharpshooters killed thousands.

Repeating rifles and crude machine-guns nicknamed coffee-mills were also used. They were called this because the cartridges were fed into the barrel from a hopper which resembled coffee-grinders. Later these were found to be dangerous for the gunners, and not very effective. Only a few were used.

At the beginning of the war, the artillery pieces were much like those which had been employed in the Napoleonic Wars. Their iron balls, some explosive, weighed from six to ten pounds. Such cannon were only accurate at ranges of about 800 yards.

As the war progressed, each side tried to build larger and more effective cannon. Robert Parrott developed what was known as the Parrott Rifle. It could hurl a ten-pound ball 4,000 yards. He also developed a siege gun whose projectiles weighed thirty pounds.

Bayonets were standard equipment on both sides. They accounted for tens of thousands of deaths. But perhaps the greatest cause of death resulted from the absolute dedication of each side—especially at the beginning. Many were as dedicated as Major Sullivan Ballou of the North. A week before he was killed at Manassas, he wrote to his wife:

> *I cannot describe to you the depths of my feelings on this*
> *calm Sabbath Night, when two thousand men are sleeping*
> *around me, many of them enjoying perhaps the last sleep before*
> *that of death, while I am suspicious that death is creeping*
> *around me with his fatal dart, as I sit communing with God,*
> *my Country and thee. . . .*
>   *Sarah my love for you is deathless, it seems to bind me*
> *with mighty cables that nothing but Omnipotence could break;*
> *and yet my love of Country comes over me like a strong wind*
> *and burns me irresistibly on with all these chains to the*
> *battlefield.*

The South was equally dedicated. Many pastors resigned their congregations and dressed in gray. Some enthusiastic ministers even led men into battle. One clergyman in charge of a section of artillery, named four of the cannon Matthew, Mark, Luke, and John. After ordering them loaded, he customarily waited until all was ready, then after lifting his hands heavenward, shouted in a stentorian voice: "In the name of the Lord, fire!" After the guns fired, he raised his hands again. This time his voice trembled with compassion, as he generously added: "And Lord, have mercy on their souls!"

Both the North and the South relied heavily on music to inspire their men. After witnessing a skirmish during the early days of the war, Julia Ward Howe was awakened in the middle of the night with the words of a poem beating at her heart. She turned on a light immediately and scribbled them on a scrap of paper for fear they might be forgotten by morning.

Liking the five verses, the "Atlantic Monthly" mailed her a check for $5. The published verses and the words caught on. Employing the same rhythmic tune that was used with John Brown's Body, almost the entire North began singing the "Battle Hymn of the Republic." The first verse was indeed a stirring one:

Mine eyes have seen the glory of the coming of
the Lord:
He is trampling out the vintage where the grapes
of wrath are stored;
He hath loosed the fateful lightning of His terrible
swift sword;
His truth is marching on.

And so, while the South sang "Dixie," the North responded with the "Battle Hymn of the Republic."

Altogether, the Union had 618 bands and since each band was composed of twenty-one musicians, there was one musician for every forty-one soldiers. The Confederates also had their bands and during the Battle of Gettysburg, they played so loudly they drew fire from the Union forces.

Realizing that both sides were frequently bored with endless days of inactivity, bouts of discouragement, acute loneliness, and sometimes utter despair, song writers kept busy. Most of their productions were sentimental. But many were extremely popular in both the North and the South. From their pens came:

Tramp! Tramp! Tramp!
Marching Through Georgia
The Girl I Left Behind Me
Tenting on the Old Camp Grund
The Battle Cry of Freedom
Just Before the Battle, Mother

Frequently an incident in the fighting inspired a writer to compose a hymn or chorus that became popular in religious circles. Such an incident happened at Allatoona Pass in Georgia. Union General J. M. Corse found himself isolated there with 1500 men, guarding vast supplies of rations.

Early one morning a Confederate Army of 6500 attacked. An artillery of twelve guns began to fire on the Federal Forts. After an hour of bombardment, Confederate General French requested that Corse surrender in order to avoid "needless effusion of blood." Moreover, he demanded that Corse surrender in five minutes.

Corse replied immediately: "Your communication demanding surrender of my command I acknowledge receipt of, and respectfully reply that we are prepared for 'the needless effusion of blood' whenever it is agreeable to you. I am, very respectfully, your obedient servant."

As he considered his plight, Corse noticed a flag signaling from Kennesaw Mountain. The message . was:

Sherman is moving with force. Hold out.

Corse held out, and even though he suffered 705 casualties and had 200 men taken prisoner, he refused to hoist the white flag. As Sherman approached, he signaled, "Are you wounded?"

Corse replied:

I am short a cheekbone and one ear, but am able to whip all hell yet.

Even though his telegraph wires had been cut, Corse held out, help came, and the Confederates withdrew.

Thoroughly inspired, Philip Bliss composed a hymn:

> *Ho, my comrades! see the signal*
> *Waving in the sky!*
> *Reinforcements now appearing,*
> *Victory is nigh.*

"Hold the fort, for I am coming!" Jesus signals still!
Wave the answer back to heaven, "By Thy grace we will!"

With such forces pushing them, brave men in both the North and the South were willing to die. And they died.

Sometimes the manner of death was even worse than the death itself. In many cases the wounded, due to the pace of the action, were left to die. Hundreds were burned to death in flames of forests or patches of brush. Surgeons were usually available, and they tried desperately to save lives, but they were hindered by crude equipment; and they were overloaded with work, sometimes having to care for the wounded and dying for eighteen to twenty-four hours at a stretch. But the surgeons on both sides did what they could, and so did the nurses. Clara Barton became especially loved. Grateful soldiers called her "Angel of the Battlefield."

Death, disease, fires, suffering and all the horrors of war accompanied the continuing battles. And these battles took place in many parts of America, including Arizona, New Mexico, Utah, Idaho, Washington, Vermont, Illinois and Minnesota.

Over half a million died, and more than half of the deaths in every camp resulted from diseases such as measles, smallpox and tuberculosis, which were spread because of indescribable sanitary conditions.

Details of the events of those gruesome and shocking years are rightfully described as an "encyclopedia of horrors."

19

Fatal Shots

Like almost everyone, Jackson at first believed that the War would be over in ninety days. Then, weeks before Manassas, George B. McClellan invaded western Virginia; and, somewhat to Jackson's despair most of the people greeted Little Mac as a hero. Worse yet, that section of Virginia decided to become a separate state and join the Union! As they awaited the approval of Congress, thousands of Virginians enlisted in the Union army.

To all the Confederacy this was a vicious blow. It was especially hard for Stonewall since many people in Clarksburg, his birthplace, and Jackson's Mills where he had played as a boy, supported the Stars and Stripes. His own sister, Laura, boasted that she would take care of the hospitalized Federals as fast as her brother wounded them.

Sometimes when Jackson couldn't sleep he wondered if his sister was right. He remembered how the North had been upset when the Supreme Court decided that the Missouri Compromise was unconstitutional and that Dred Scott was still a slave. *What the North didn't seem to realize was that Taney like many other Southerners had freed his own slaves, and that soon after the decision, the owner of Dred Scott had freed him.*

The war, Jackson was convinced, was not being fought over slavery, but over the right of states to secede. Furthermore, if western Virginia could secede from Virginia, why couldn't Virginia secede from the Union?

He still believed that slavery would eventually come to an end. Britain had freed her slaves without bloodshed, and so had France. Why couldn't the United States do the same? He became more than ever determined to do his part to win the war, and to win it as soon as possible.

The chiefs of staff on both sides viewed the war like chess players viewing a game of chess. And, like chess players, they studied each move with great care. Even before Virginia seceded, Lincoln had declared a blockade of southern ports. This blockade, a part of Old Fuss and Feathers' Anaconda Plan, was designed to keep arms and supplies from flowing into the South, and to stop cotton, their big cash crop, from flowing *out* of the South. The North had a large navy to carry out this plan.

Inspired by McClellan's success in western Virginia—many called him The Little Napoleon—he was made the head of the Union armies. Auburn-haired Little Mac then got busy and formed what he named The Army of the Potomac. He tirelessly organized and drilled his men.

Northern newspapers became restless. "On to Richmond!" they screamed.

But what was the best way to take Richmond?

Many thought the best way was to march straight across Virginia, and take it by frontal attack. After all, it was only one hundred miles away. McClellan, however, shook his head. "Crossing Virginia, is not as easy as it seems," he explained. He pointed to a map. "You see, we'd have to cross four rivers: the Rappahannock, the Mattapony, the Panmunkey, and the Chickahominy; and since the Rebels would have the time, they'd blow up all the bridges." He took a deep breath and unfolded another map.

"I have a better plan. Let's send our army down the Potomac, into Chesapeake Bay. Then, at Fort Monroe—and please remember that solid fort is still in Federal hands—we'll turn North, go up the peninsula between the James and York rivers, and hit 'em on their soft underside. Richmond is only eighty miles from Fort Monroe. We could even make use of the James River."

Lincoln, along with others, was not enthusiastic about this strategy, but McClellan finally got their consent. Then someone dashed cold water over the plan. "It's true that we have a better navy than the South. But remember, they have that dreadful iron-clad *Merrimac*! It could sink our transports in no time."

The entire North knew about the *Merrimac*, the world's first iron-clad battleship. Its heavy steel ram could be jammed through the underwater hulls of other ships and send them to Davy Jones' Locker in no time. Normal shells glanced off her sides with no more effect than peas from a popgun.

The North, then, built a rival battleship—the *Monitor*, which was also protected with heavy iron sides. The *Merrimac* was larger. The *Monitor* was more agile. The *Merrimac's* hull was twenty-two feet below the surface, while the *Monitor's* hull was only ten and a half feet below the surface. Thus the *Monitor* could move in shallower water than the *Merrimac*.

The *Merrimac* had ten guns. The *Monitor* had only two guns. But her guns were in a revolving turret which could easily be turned, while the *Merrimac's* guns were all but stationary. The *Monitor*, however, could only fire once every eight minutes, while the *Merrimac* could fire much faster.

The *Monitor's* supreme advantage was that it was so low in the water is was called "a cheese box on a raft." This made it a difficult target.

On Sunday morning, March 9, 1862, the two ironclads met one another in battle just north of Norfolk, Virginia. Union men from the Fort watched with great fear. If the *Merrimac* were to sink the *Monitor*, all their ships would be in peril.

At one point, armed men from the *Merrimac* tried to board the *Monitor*. But the agile *Monitor* was able to make a quick turn and get away.

After four hours of constant fighting, the rivals parted. The *Merrimac* went on to other battles until she needed repairs and was sent into dry dock.

When McClellan learned of this through his network of spies, he launched a massive move with his army down the Potomac. President Lincoln asked that 30,000 men remain in Washington to protect the city, and that left 100,000 for McClellan's Peninsular Campaign. The troops boarded 113 steamships and 88 barges and hoped that the *Merrimac* would not be repaired before they landed safely at Fort Monroe.

Robert E. Lee, realized that the threat to Washington was weakening McClellan's advance toward Richmond, and he decided to create even more problems. In a bold move, he ordered Jackson to invade Virginia. This would ensure that the troops in Washington could not join in the Peninsular Campaign.

He also decreed that Jackson would have to give

up the "Stonewall Brigade", and assume command of a new army in Virginia. November 4, 1861 was the day of parting. As his old brigade stood at attention, Jackson rode up on Little Sorrel. As usual, his clothes were not in perfect shape. His faded coat was a relic of the Mexican War. His cap was worn and out of shape, and the visor slanted toward his nose.

Awkward Francis Marion, the Swamp Fox, once was forced to give up his bridgade. Now his admirer, Jackson, in a high-pitched voice, began:

"Officers and men of the First Brigade, I am not here to make a speech but simply to say farewell. I met you at Harpers Ferry in the commencement of the War, and I cannot leave you without giving expression to my admiration of your conduct from that day to this, whether on the march, in the bivouac, or on the bloody plains of Mannasas. I shall look forward with great anxiety to your future movements, and I trust whenever I hear of the First Brigade on the field of battle it will still be of nobler deeds achieved and higher reputation won.

"In the Army of Shenandoah you were the First Brigade; in the Army of the Potomac you were the First Brigade; in the Second Corps of this army you are the First Brigade; you are the First Brigade in the affections of your general; and I hope by your future deeds and bearing you will be handed down to posterity as the First Brigade in our second War of Independence.

"Farewell!"

Jackson then touched Little Sorrel and rode away. As he sped on, his huge feet in his flop-top boots, the men sounded their farewell with a series of rebel yells.

All at once Stonewall was overcome with emotion. His eyes flooded and tears streamed down his cheeks.

But controlling himself with his iron will, he prepared to make things difficult for his old classmate, Major General Henry B. McClellan.

The Shenandoah Valley with its streams, beautiful roads, manicured farms, Mennonite and Dunkard meetinghouses, was one of the most prosperous and significant valleys in the world. Writing to a friend, Jackson was emphatic: "If this valley is lost, Virginia is lost."

Jackson had two plans for keeping Virginia. He would inspire his men with Christian fervor; and he would follow his old military motto which was simple and to the point:

Always mystify, mislead, and surprise the enemy, if possible; and when you strike and overcome him, never give up the pursuit as long as your men have strength to follow; for an army routed, if hotly pursued, becomes panic-stricken and can then be destroyed by half their number.

Although it was winter, Jackson led his army on long marches, the destination of which he never mentioned to anyone. His men seldom minded. They knew that Old Jack was out to mystify the enemy. And mystify them, he did.

The Federals tried to follow him, but he eluded them. Then in an unexpected place and in an unexpected manner, he confronted them. Although he often fought against overwhelming odds, he usually won. His own army respected him, and so did the enemy. Northern newspapers spoke of his determination, solid Christianity and military genius. Some compared him to Hannibal. Union prisoners bragged: "We were captured by Stonewall Jackson's brigade!"

While Jackson was wearing out the Federals in Virginia, Little Mac managed to land his troops at

Fort Monroe. The *Merrimac*, would no longer threaten him because she was scuttled when she faced overwhelming odds.

The *Monitor*, also, had a short life. It sank in a storm that lashed Cape Hatteras, North Carolina.

After landing, instead of heading for Richmond, Little Mac lay siege to Yorktown. For a full month his cannon boomed and the Confederates used that time to reinforce Richmond's fortifications. Then one morning the Yanks awakened and were horrified to learn that Yorktown's defenders had escaped during the night.

This meant that Little Mac had wasted a month's time; and more troops were now defending Richmond. Moreover, his right flank was exposed just north of the Chickahominy. General Lee was in that area and he ordered Stonewall Jackson to join him.

Fierce battles followed. McClellan was forced to retreat across a swamp. In spite of great loss of life, little Mac headed for Richmond. He got within six miles of his goal.

His army astraddle the Chickahominy, ever-cautious McClellan waited for the Washington troops to help him. But Lincoln would not allow them to go. Instead, he ordered McClellan to return to Northern Virginia. The invincible Army of the Potomac had failed. Much blood had been shed. At this discouraging time, Brigadier General Daniel Butterfield, a Union commander, composed the mournful bugle call known as *Taps*.

The Peninsular Campaign was over.

Now that Richmond was safe, Stonewall attended church on Sunday. Well-wishers mobbed him and eulogized him. His response to this adoration was the same as always: "All the glory belongs to God."

He also solemnly warned that it would be sinful and disastrous for anyone to glory in his own success.

As the cold of December settled over the North, it became apparent that the armies of both the North and the South were becoming weary and, sometimes, friendly with one another.

Both sides loved music; and during a pause while exchanging fire across a river, a Yankee might shout: Hey Johnny Reb, give us some music. Then, while both sides held their fire, a Southern band would strike up with "Dixie". The Yanks would reply with "The Battle Hymn of the Republic."

The Southerners had a good cornet player. Amidst heavy firing, a Federal picket called across no-man's-land. "Hey, Johnny! We want to hear that cornet."

"He's afraid you'll damage his horn."

"We'll hold fire."

"All right, here he is."

Favorite hymns in both camps were: "Amazing Grace," "Just As I Am," "When I Survey The Wondrous Cross," and "There Is a Fountain Filled With Blood."

Stonewall Jackson promoted revivals. A private wrote from his camp in Virginia:

> *We are having a glorious time . . . we commenced a protracted meeting in this brigade about four days ago, Gen. Jackson (God bless him) has given us the privilege to be exempt from Morning Drill in order that we may attend preaching.*

Another soldier wrote from Louisiana: "A revival of religion has commenced in camp. I never saw such a difference in men in my life. There is but one man to my knowledge who makes a regular business of swearing. When I first came out in the army we could scarcely hear anything but profanity. Over 250 have been converted since last summer."

During a revival, when a man asked to be baptized,

someone shouted, "Let's quit shootin' until we baptize one of our'n new converts."

The firing stopped, and as Private Goodwin was being immersed, both sides joined in singing "There is a Fountain Filled With Blood." After Goodwin stepped ashore the firing resumed.

Stonewall never used his sword, so the blade rusted. This was not true of his Bible. He read it every day.

That winter, Stonewall received the wonderful news that his wife had given birth to a little girl. Beside himself with joy, he wrote to Anna: "Give the baby daughter a shower of kisses from her father, and tell her he loves her better that all the baby boys in the world."

Her name was Julia, in honor of Stonewall's mother.

But he didn't have time to pay Julia a visit. Less than three weeks later he and General Lee faced 115,000 Union soldiers across the Rappahannock River at Fredericksburg. The battle was a bloodbath. The Union lost 12,600 men, and the victorious Confederates an additional 5,300.

As winter thawed and changed into spring, Jackson had a feeling that he would soon be engaged in the greatest battle of his life. The blockade was working. Supplies were short. People were hungry. General Lee was restless. Fighting Joe Hooker was determined to crush Lee somewhere in Virginia, to make himself a hero—and end the War. Joe was so addicted to the bottle, his men composed and sang a ditty about him.

Joe Hooker is our leader—
He takes his whiskey strong!
He was commander of the Army of the Potomac, His task: Win the War!

Hooker's army had wintered on the north side of

the Rappahannock. Jackson and Lee, along with other commanders, made camp on the southern side of the same river.

As the snow melted and the river warmed, each army waited for the other to make a move. Enemy pickets often called across the stream to one another. They communicated by means of tiny sailboats loaded with presents. Hooker's men usually sent tobacco while the Yanks responded with candy, books, or family pictures.

Each side studied the other by means of balloons. When the peach and cherry trees began to bloom, Jackson knew that a new torrent of blood was about to be shed. In the calm before the inevitable storm, he sent word to Anna to come for a visit.

In the midst of a rainstorm, Anna and little Julia arrived. It was hard for Stonewall to put his daughter down. Holding her to a mirror, he said, "Now Miss Jackson, take a good look at yourself."

For nine days, Stonewall spent every spare moment with his family. Fearing that this might be the last time she could get a professional photograph of her husband, Anna arranged for one. After the camera clicked, she remarked that she had never seen him in better condition.

He was 39 years old.

Early in the morning of April 29, 1863, Jackson was awakened by a messenger. "Hooker is crossing the river," he announced.

While Anna prepared to leave for Richmond, guns started to rattle. Soon there were lines of wounded, some on stretchers, on their way to the hospital. Anna said to the chaplain who was taking her to the train, "I agree with Tom that war is hell."

Fighting Joe was confident. He had 133,000 men

and 404 cannon, while Lee had only 60,000 men and 228 cannon. Pointing to a spot on the map named Chancellorsville, he said, "If I can put my army there, God Almighty cannot drive me out." With his superior forces, it seemed that he could not possibly lose.

Lee and Jackson, however, knew that Fighting Joe lacked courage, was easily surprised, and easily intimidated. The two generals entered a clump of woods. Sitting on hardtack boxes with a map before them, they plotted their strategy. Jackson ran his finger along a map. "See this road? It leads around Hooker's flank."

Jackson had learned about that road through diligent inquiry. He had told Chaplain Lacy about his need of a road that would lead to Hooker's flank, and Lacy had outlined such a road on a map.

Jackson frowned. "That's too close to the Federal lines," he objected. "We need a more distant one." Lacy bit his lip. "Colonel Wellford, owner of Catherine Furnace, will know of such a road,"

The Colonel indicated where a more distant road led, and Jackson decided it was a better plan. The Colonel's son agreed to lead the way, and Jackson's mapmaker drew a map which the Generals now studied.

"We'll follow this road," explained Jackson, "then we'll pounce on his right flank."

"And what will you make this movement with?" asked Lee.

"With my whole corps."

Lee's eyes widened. "And what will you leave me?"

"The divisions of Anderson and McClaws."

Lee paused. Jackson's plan meant that he would have about 26,000 men, while Lee would only have a mere 14,000 to be arrayed head-on against Hooker's 75,000.

It was incredible. But Lee had confidence in Jackson, and so he replied, "Well, go on."

Jackson's men were instructed to be silent, and were warned that stragglers would be prodded with a bayonet. At dawn 26,000 soldiers started out. The column was ten miles long, and it moved slowly. The Federals spotted them, but Hooker assumed they were retreating. Lee had the job of appearing strong so Hooker would not go after Jackson. He instructed Anderson and McClaws to periodically fire their muskets at the Federals. And he opened up with his own artillery.

His big feet drooping in the sides of Little Sorrel, Jackson kept moving up and down the columns, and repeating:

"Press on. Press on."

Zero hour came at 5:15. Jackson's corps was on the west of Hooker's right flank. "General, are you ready?" asked Jackson.

"Yes, Sir."

"You can go forward, Sir," replied Jackson.

Bugles sounded. The men dashed toward the enemy screaming the Rebel Yell with all the power their vocal chords and lungs could manage. Overwhelmed, the Yanks threw down their arms and fled. Officers tried to stop the flight. General Howard stood weeping in the middle of the road. Although wounded, he embraced a Union flag that a regiment had deserted, and pled with the men to stand firm.

Darkness, fell, and Jackson's men unfamiliar with the terrain, became disorganized. Pressing this advantage, the Federals began a heavy artillery barrage. As their grape swept the road, and a bright moon lit the area, Jackson and some of his officers searched

the area, seeking to discover the lay of the land.

Suddenly there was a shot from a pocket of Confederates. It was followed by a volley of shots. Two of Jackson's officers were killed and Jackson was wounded. Little Sorrel bolted into the bushes, thus pushing Jackson off and scratching his face.

Alarmed, an officer shouted, "Cease firing. You're firing at your own men!"

The firing stopped, but it was too late. Stonewall had been dreadfully wounded in the arm. James Power Smith, an aide, cut open the coat sleeve, and with his handkerchief bound the arm above the wound to stop the flow of blood. Messengers ran to inform Dr. Hunter McGuire, the surgeon, and soldiers were brought from the line nearby to be litter bearers. They placed the General upon a litter and quietly and carefully carried Stonewall off the battlefield. He had been shot by one of his own men.

20

The Final River

"Stonewall, I hope you're not badly hurt," said McGuire, anxiously bending over him.

"I fear I'm dying," groaned Jackson, biting his lip.

While the doctor was checking him, Lieutenant Morrison was sent to Richmond to escort Anna to his side. After the checking, and in the midst of the thunder of firing guns, the doctor said, "I'm afraid, General, that we'll have to amputate your left arm."

"Very well," replied Jackson.

Chloroform was pressed to his nose, and Jackson mumbled, "What an infinite blessing... blessing...blessing...bless..." He then fell into unconsciousness. His arm was removed.

A note from General Lee arrived. It said:

Give him my affectionate regards, and tell him to make haste and come back to me as soon as he can. He has lost his left arm but I have lost my right arm.

The wounded general, together with his wife and daughter, were moved as soon as possible to Guinea

Station far to the rear of the battlefront. Another note from Lee arrived. Anna read it out loud: "Could I have directed events, I should have chosen for the good of the country, to have been disabled in your stead. I congratulate you on the victory which is due to your skill and energy."

Jackson was pleased, and yet even before Anna laid the note down, he commented: "General Lee is very kind, but he should give the glory to God."

Jackson slept soundly on Saturday night, and Sunday Chaplain Lacy came to visit. Seeing the stump of his left arm, Lacy exclaimed: "Oh, General, what a calamity!"

Jackson smiled at his old friend. Then he replied: "I believe it has been done according to God's holy will, and I acquiesce entirely to it. You may think it strange; but you never saw me more perfectly contented than I am today; for I am sure that my Heavenly Father designs this affliction for my good. I can wait until God, in His own time, shall make known to me the object He has in thus afflicting me. If it were in my power to replace my arm, I would not dare do it, unless I could know it was the will of the Heavenly Father."

He arranged for the chaplain to visit him every day at 10 a.m. and join with him in Bible study.

Jackson's arm was healing, but he developed a heavy cold. The cold worsened and turned into pneumonia. During the week his condition grew worse. By Saturday it appeared that he would not live. That evening, Anna, along with her brother, read the 51st Psalm to him. Then, knowing that the Doxology was a favorite of his, they sang it for him.

On the next day, May 10, it was clear that the General had but a few hours to live. Chaplain Lacy said that he would spend the day with him, but

Jackson replied: "No, it would be better for you to preach to the men."

Later, while in delirium, he gave orders to General A.P. Hill. "Order them to attack! Call up the reserves!" Then he became quiet. The doctors told Anna she should inform him when he was about to pass away. She now did so as tenderly as possible. Smiling up at Anna, he responded, "My wish is fulfilled. I've always wanted to die on Sunday."

At 3:15 his face relaxed. Utterly calm, he distinctly murmured: "Let us cross over the river and rest under the shade of the trees." This time it was not the Rappahannock, the Potomac, or the Chickahominy. It was the Jordan, that mystical river that flows between mortality and immortality.

Jackson's body was taken to Richmond, with 20,000 mourners following in the funeral procession. Next it was sent to Lexington. Students there carried it to the Virginia Military Institute where it lay in state in the lecture room in which Jackson had taught. The funeral sermon was delivered by Doctor White, and then the mighty Stonewall Jackson was buried in the town cemetery.

In Washington on May 13, 1863, *The Daily Chronicle* printed an article by John Forney titled "The Death of Stonewall Jackson." it read:

> Stonewall Jackson is dead. While we are only too glad to be rid, in a way, of so terrible a foe, our sense of relief is not unmingled with emotions of sorrow and sympathy at the death of so brave a man. Every man who possesses the least particle of magnanimity must admire the qualities for which Stonewall Jackson was celebrated—his heroism, his bravery, his sublime devotion, his purity of character. . . Stonewall Jackson was a great general, a noble Christian and a pure man. May God throw these great virtues

against the sins of the secessionists, the advocates of
a great national crime.

Among the thousands who read the article was
President Lincoln. He wrote to Forney: ''I wish to
lose no time in thanking you for your excellent and
manly article in the *Chronicle* on Jackson.''

The war continued to rage for two more years.
There were terrible battles and much bloodshed. Then
on April 9, 1865, Robert E. Lee sent word to Ulysses
S. Grant that he would like to meet him for an
interview. This was the beginning of the end.

The two generals met in the village of Appomattox
Court House on April 9, to agree on terms for the
surrender of all Confederate forces in the field. As Lee
signed the papers, Wilmer McClean, in whose home
they met, made a sage remark: ''The war started in

my kitchen and ended in my parlor.'' Those who understood, smiled. They remembered that during the First Battle of Manassas, a Union shell had fallen down his chimney into a pot of stew in his kitchen. Then in the Second Battle of Manassas, he was so annoyed by the soldiers who tramped over his fine lawns, he moved to this little town of Appomatox Court House, where he felt sure he would be at a safe distance from all fighting. It was on this spot that papers were signed. The War was over.

Five days later—April 14, 1865, Abraham Lincoln was assassinated. Both North and South were in turmoil.

Time began its healing, but the battles were not forgotten. Some years later, the Jackson Monument was erected in Richmond's Capital Square and a group of old men slept around the monument.

''What are you doing here?'' asked a curious man.

''We were *his* boys,'' exclaimed an almost toothless man. ''We just wanted to be with Old Jack again.''

The rest of America remembers Old Jack, too. In our time we have fifty cities or counties named Jackson, plus others like Jacksonville, and many of these were named after Stonewall. We also have Stonewall Jackson Lake, Stonewall Jackson Dam, and numerous schools which bear his name.

But the most famous physical memorial to Jackson is the largest stone carving in the world on Stone Mountain just outside Atlanta. This carving features Robert E. Lee, Jefferson Davis, and Stonewall Jackson. It took fifty years to complete and measures 90 feet by 190 feet.

But Jackson's greatest memorial is the spiritual one. STONEWALL KNEW CHRIST, and JESUS CHRIST KNEW STONEWALL!

And what happened to Little Sorrel, who often slept near his master, ate apples from his hand, carried him into battle, and was with him when he was fatally wounded?

The Governor of Virginia retired him to Jackson's father-in-law's farm in North Carolina where he was admired and indulged by many. Then he was transferred to the Soldier's Home in Richmond where he received even more attention from the veterans.

Little Sorrel enjoyed his retirement. But, like a true Confederate, he believed in secession. As ingenious as before, he often removed the top rail of the fence and leaped to freedom. He also learned to unlock the gate and lead his friends to greener pastures. He died at about the age of 30 and today his remains may be viewed at the Virginia Military Institute Museum in Lexington.

"THERE STANDS JACKSON LIKE A STONE WALL."

ON THIS SPOT
FELL
MORTALLY WOUNDED
THOMAS J. JACKSON
Lt. Gen. C.S.A.
May 2nd 1863

JACKSON

*Stone Mountain Memorial, Atlanta, Georgia. Largest exposed
granite mountain in the world—190ft. x 305 ft.*

IMPORTANT EVENTS

1824   On January 21 Thomas Jackson was born.

1827   Tom's sister Elizabeth and his father Jonathan died.

Tom's sister Laura Ann was born.

1829   Andrew Jackson became President.

1830   Tom's mother Julia married Blake Woodson.

1831   Tom and Laura Ann were sent to live with relatives.

Tom's half-brother William Wirt was born to Julia.

Tom's mother Julia died.

1832   Tom went to live with Cummins Jackson.

1836   Tom and Warren sold firewood on the Ohio and Mississippi Rivers.

1841   Tom became a constable.

Tom's brother Warren died of tuberculosis.

1842   Tom was accepted at West Point.

Tom changed his name to Thomas Jonathan Jackson.

1845   James Polk became President.

1846   Tom graduated from West Point and was assigned to Point Isabel.

1847   Jackson distinguished himself at Chapultepec.

1848   Treaty with Mexico was signed on February 2.

1849	Jackson was baptized on April 29.
1851	Jackson became a professor at Virginia Military Institute.
	Jackson joined the Presbyterian Church.
1853	Jackson married Elinor Junkin.
1854	Elinor and her new baby died.
1855	Jackson started Sunday school for slaves.
1856	Jackson sailed for Europe.
1857	Jackson was elected deacon.
	The Supreme Court decided the Missouri Compromise was unconstitutional and Dred Scott was still a slave.
	Jackson married Anna Morrison.
1859	John Brown was hanged for the killings at Harpers Ferry.
1860	Abraham Lincoln was elected President.
1861	The War between the states began.
1863	In the battle of Chancelorsville (May 2-4) Stonewall Jackson was shot. He died May 10.
1865	Lee surrendered on April 9, ending the War.
1865	President Abraham Lincoln was assassinated April 14.

BIBLIOGRAPHY

Bailey, Ronald H., *The Battle of Antietam*, (Time-Life Books, 1984).

Bell, Irvin Wiley, *The Life of Johnny, Reb.* (Bobs-Merrill, 1943).

Brockett, L.P. *Our Great Captains*, (Charles B. Richardson, 1866).

Catton, William and Bruce, *Two Roads To Sumter,* (McGraw Hill, 1963).

Condon, Don, *Combat, The Civil War*, (Delacorte Press, 1967).

Dabney, R.L., *Life Campaigns of T. J. Jackson*, (Sprinkle Publications, 1983).

Davis, Burke, *The Civil War, Strange* and *Fascinating Facts*, (Fairfax Press, 1982).

Davis, Burke, *They Called Him Stonewall*, (Holt, Rinehart & Winston, 1954).

Davis, William C., *Fort Sumter to Bull Run*, (Time-Life Books, 1983).

Douglas, Henry Kid, *I Rode With Stonewall*, (Universty of North Carolina Press), 1940

Editors, The, *The Blockade* (Time-Life Books, 1983).

Edmonds, Franklin F. *Ulysses S. Grant* (George W. Jacobs, 1915).

Frassanito, William A., *Antietam*, (Scribners, 1978).

Freeman, Douglas Southall, *Lee's Lieutenants, Vol. 1, 2, 3.* (Scribners, 1943).

Fritz, Jean, *Stonewall*, (Putnam, 1879).

Fuller, Claude E., *Firearms of the Confederacy*, (Quarterman Publications, 1944).

Gregory, Jaynes, *Wilderness to Cold Harbor*, (Time-Life Books, 1986).

Goodrick, William K., Fredericksburg to Chancellorsville, (Time-Life Books, 1985).

Jones, William J. D. D. *Christ in the Camp*, (Sprinkle Publications, 1986).

Ludwig, Charles *Champion of Freedom*, (Bethany House, 1987).

Mansfield, Edward D., *Life of General Winfield Scott, (A.S. Barnes & Co., 1848).*

Neven, David, *Atlanta to the Sea*, (Time-Life Books, 1986).

Rankin, Hugh F., *Francis Marion: the Swamp Fox*, (Thomas Crowell, 1937).

Richards, Warren J., *God Blessed Our Arms With Victory* (Vantage Press, 1986).

Robertson, James I. Jr., *The Soldier's Life*, Time-Life Books, 1984).

Sandburg, Carl, *Abraham Lincoln : Prairie Years*, Vol. *1. 2.*, (Scribners, 1926). *Abraham Lincoln: War Years*, *Vol. 1.2. 3.*, Scribners, 1939).

Smith, Arthur D. Howden, *Old Fuss And Feathers*, (The Greystone Press, 1937).

Smith, Charles W., *Roger B. Taney, Jacksonian Jurist*, (De Capo Press, 1973).

Stackpole, Edward J., *Chancellorsville, Lee's Greatest Battle*, (Stackpole, 1958).

Stern, Phillip Van Doren, *When The Guns Roared*, (Doubleday, 1965).

Strode, Hudson, *Jefferson Davis American Patriot*, (Harcourt Brace, 1955).

Twain, Mark, *Mississippi Writings*, (Viking Press, 1982).

Vandrive, Frank E., *Mighty Stonewall*, (McGraw Hill, 1943).

Webb, Willard, *Crucial Moments of The Civil War, (Bonanza Books, 1981).*

Weems, M.L., *Life of Francis Marion*, (Joseph Allen, 1837).

INDEX

SOWERS SERIES